SECOND EDITION

Literacy
in the
DIGITAL
AGE

I dedicate this book to the most literate teacher I know—my wife, Jackie.

SECOND EDITION

Literacy
in the
DIGITAL
AGE

R. W. BURNISKE

Foreword by DONNA OGLE

CORWIN PRESS
A SAGE Company
Thousand Oaks, CA 91320

Originally published as *Literacy in the Cyberage: Composing Ourselves Online.*

For information:

Corwin Press
A SAGE Company
2455 Teller Road
Thousand Oaks, California 91320
www.corwinpress.com

SAGE India Pvt. Ltd.
B 1/I 1 Mohan Cooperative
 Industrial Area
Mathura Road, New Delhi 110 044
India

SAGE Ltd.
1 Oliver's Yard
55 City Road
London EC1Y 1SP
United Kingdom

SAGE Asia-Pacific Pte. Ltd.
33 Pekin Street #02-01
Far East Square
Singapore 048763

Printed in the United States of America.

Library of Congress Cataloging-in-Publication Data

Burniske, R. W., 1960–2006
Literacy in the digital age/R. W. Burniske. — 2nd ed.
    p. cm.
Rev. ed. of: Literacy in the cyberage. 2000.
Includes bibliographical references and index.
ISBN 978-1-4129-5745-8 (cloth)
ISBN 978-1-4129-5746-5 (pbk.)
    1. Computers and literacy. 2. Language arts—Computer-assisted instruction. I. Burniske, R. W., 1960–2006 Literacy in the cyberage. II. Title.

LC149.5.B87 2008
302.2'244'0285—dc22   2007033100

This book is printed on acid-free paper.

07   08   09   10   11   10   9   8   7   6   5   4   3   2   1

Acquisitions Editor:	Hudson Perigo
Editorial Assistants:	Jordan Barbakow, Lesley Blake
Production Editor:	Cassandra Margaret Seibel
Copy Editor:	Julie Gwin
Typesetter:	C&M Digitals (P) Ltd.
Proofreader:	Susan Schon
Indexer:	Sylvia Coates
Cover Designer:	Karine Hovsepian

In Tribute

R. W. "Buddy" Burniske, PhD, passed away April 20, 2006, after an 18-month struggle with cancer. He was a tenured associate professor at the University of Hawaii at Manoa, College of Education, Department of Educational Technology. Through his many published works, Buddy was able to influence thousands of people around the world through his writing and his teaching. However, Buddy was not only a teacher in the classroom, with thoughtful and creative teaching ideas, as demonstrated in this book, *Literacy in the Digital Age* (2nd edition). Buddy also taught through the example of his life.

In April 2006, Buddy entered the St. Francis Hospice with a home care program, and on April 20, 2006, he peacefully passed away in the presence of his family. On April 24, I e-mailed a message to the worldwide community that knew and loved Buddy. In the hours, days, and weeks after Buddy's death, I received many beautiful e-mail messages, letters, and cards. Family, friends, colleagues, and students thoughtfully and sincerely wrote messages of comfort and testaments to Buddy's impact on them, their lives, and their work. I include a few of those below.

> "You don't know me but I am a graduate student in ETEC and Buddy was my advisor this past year."

> "Knowing Buddy changed my life. I am a librarian who has worked at the University of Hawaii at Manoa for more than 25 years. My first adventure into educational technology was to walk into a class taught by Buddy. . . . From that day forward, how I work with people and how I view the world changed for the better, so much better."

> "I never thought I would actually experience good teaching, but then I took Dr. B's course. He was the greatest teacher I have ever had. He challenged my mind more than any other teacher, and he cared so much about me and my learning. When I think of new ideas to teach I remember what he said about 'creating a community of inquiry' and I try to model that."

> "I'm a former student of Dr. Burniske at ISKL (The International School of Kuala Lumpur). I was in the class of 1995. His teachings have lingered with me ever since I left high school. In college, I decided to reread the books he assigned us in [Advanced Placement] English that I, regrettably, didn't always understand.

Yet I knew he assigned them for a reason, and perhaps I just needed the maturity to appreciate them; so I reread books like Wharton's *The House of Mirth* and Tanizaki's *The Makioka Sisters*. His influence persists even now, as I pursue my doctorate degree in education, and explore how technologies can be used to enhance education. But more than anything, he taught me how to be open-minded, critical, self-reflecting, and passionate about my work."

"Buddy in his friendship gave me the ultimate teacher's gift in his surpassing wisdom and passion and humanity. It's fair to say he became my mentor at the last."

To learn more about Buddy, you can search on YouTube.com for *Burniske* and see videos posted there, including Buddy narrating a children's story he wrote entitled *Clarence the Turtle*.

Jackie Burniske
Honolulu, Hawaii 2007

Contents

Foreword

The Digital Age has arrived, and with it, e-mail, blogs, World Wide Web access, unedited information and misinformation, hackers, and an incredible range of communication possibilities, both locally and internationally. We as literacy educators have no choice but to accept our responsibility to help students negotiate these new forms of communication. Although some of us may still feel inadequate when using computers, especially regarding the technical skills needed to take advantage of the myriad of possibilities that confront us, we do know a great deal about communication. It is this expertise that is desperately needed by young Digital Age enthusiasts. How can they determine the author of texts? How can they construct the meaning contained in electronic messages? How can they identify the subtle emotional intents and messages contained in the visual and verbal presentations? How can they most honestly and effectively present themselves and their ideas to audiences they meet electronically? How can we, their teachers, most effectively guide them in reading, responding to, and composing messages?

On my way to the library in an elementary school recently, I became intrigued by the hall bulletin board. At the top was the question, "What do we mean when we say appropriate use of the Internet?" Large sheets of paper contained lists of students' responses to the question. Heading their lists were: Don't use chat rooms without teacher's permission, don't be mean, don't send viruses, no swearing, don't chat with strangers, no naughty sites, don't give out personal information, and don't pretend to be someone else. These statements of caution by children sobered me. What responsibilities this generation of young people has to assume. Every form of seduction and persuasion can be accessed easily via the computer. Students are more vulnerable than ever before to unidentified and unregulated messages, and they have all the more reason to take literacy seriously—what an opportunity to explore with them key concepts like authorship, voice, and critical evaluation.

They also have access to an incredibly rich resource via electronic communication with people across the globe and information and documents unavailable locally. The new technology enables them to collaborate in new ways in researching, writing, illustrating, and presenting information and ideas. They deserve teachers who can help them use this potential effectively.

Into this new reality comes R. W. Burniske's refreshing message to literacy educators. What a treat it is to read! Here is a book that puts the possibilities of computers in perspective for literacy educators. Burniske examines both the potential and problems of the Digital Age technologies for literacy educators. Instead of a technologically focused guide, this book takes a philosophical and communications perspective. Readers are challenged to expand our concept of "literacy" as we follow his examination of the various aspects of literacy from civil to pedagogical. Burniske has constructed a wonderful bridge for us and leads us to the new age by building on what we know and do well. He shows us how to expand our instruction so that electronic literacy becomes an essential component of our classrooms. He challenges us to realize our commitment to develop our students as critical and reflective language users. In the process, both our students and we, their teachers, will compose ourselves online.

This is a book all serious literacy professionals need to read and discuss with colleagues. My thanks to Burniske for providing such an inviting guidebook for the journey.

Donna Ogle
President, International Reading Association, 2001–2002
Professor of Reading and Language
National-Louis University
Chicago, Illinois

About the Author

Richard "Buddy" William Burniske, PhD
February 27, 1960–April 20, 2006, Honolulu, HI

R. W. Burniske grew up in West Hatfield, Massachusetts, attending Hatfield schools from Grades 1 through 8, graduating from Deerfield Academy in Deerfield, Massachusetts, in 1978.

He accepted a John Motley Morehead Scholarship to the University of North Carolina at Chapel Hill. In addition to full tuition, the scholarship provided summer enrichment programs. As a result, he spent the summer of 1978 hiking in Colorado, 1979 with the Los Angeles Police Department, 1980 in New York City as an intern with E.P. Dutton and the *Paris Review*, and 1981 in Monrovia, Liberia. He graduated in 1982, earning a BA in English with Honors in Creative Writing.

Having married in 1982, he and his wife jointly worked at the Cairo American College. They left Egypt in June of 1983 and returned to Massachusetts, where Dr. Burniske taught English and was the Director of Student Activities at Deerfield Academy from 1983 to 1987. Each summer, he pursued his master's degree from the Bread Loaf School of English in Vermont.

Dr. Burniske and his family left Deerfield for Quito, Ecuador, in August of 1987 to teach at Academia Cotopaxi. He started as an English teacher, became dean of students, and then assistant principal. In the summers, he studied, and he was awarded his MA in English literature from Lincoln College in Oxford, England, in 1989.

In August of 1992, the Burniske family departed Ecuador for Malaysia, where he and his wife taught at the International School of Kuala Lumpur for the next four years. His interest in the Internet and conducting technology projects with his students began in Malaysia.

In 1996, they all moved to Austin, Texas, where Dr. Burniske began work on his doctoral degree at the University of Texas. While he was pursuing his doctorate, he became involved with a program initiated by the World Bank Institute designed to help teachers in developing countries learn how to use computer technology for teaching and learning purposes. He soon became the director of professional development, writing a curriculum and field testing it in Africa, Asia, the Middle East, and the Americas. He received his PhD in computers and English studies in May of 2002 from the University of Texas, and he accepted a position as a professor at the University of Hawaii, where he was awarded tenure in 2005. Dr. Burniske has published numerous books, articles, and Web sites, including *Breaking Down the Digital Walls: Learning to Teach in a Post-modem*

World (Albany, 2001), and *Literacy in the Cyberage: Composing Ourselves Online* (2000).

His far-reaching impact on his students, colleagues, and readers will be felt for many years to come. With this publication of a second edition of *Literacy in the Cyberage*, we hope *Literacy in the Digital Age* will shed light on Dr. Burniske's educational innovations and amplify his legacy.

Introduction

Literacy: Ask 5 people to define this term and you're likely to hear 10 different answers. That's what happens, though, when a word develops a split personality. On one hand, literacy conjures images of the technical skills required to read and write, the denotation that the U.S. Army reinforced when it coined the term *functional literacy* during World War II. This line of thinking, as a number of literacy experts have noted, bred the ideas of "survival literacy" and "basic literacy" (de Castell & Maclennon, 1989, p. 7). However, the second strain of literacy, *critical literacy*, vexes the conversation far more today because of its many connotations, most of which stem from the idea of what it means to be educated. Whereas functional literacy lends itself to standardized tests that measure skills of one kind or another, it is clearly more difficult to determine when someone has acquired the critical literacy that describes "a liberally educated or learned person" (*New Shorter Oxford English Dictionary*, 1993, p. 1604). It's little wonder, then, that five respondents would hedge their bets, offering definitions that address both specific, technical skills and the more nebulous qualities that would fully describe the literate individual.

Although functional literacy remains a prerequisite for other types of literacy, it is not the primary focus of this book. Of course, educators still need to teach students how to read and write while incorporating new technology into their classrooms, but they also need to teach them how to interpret and contextualize the words and information they encounter in electronic mail, discussion forums, Web sites, and more. Unfortunately, many how-to books dedicated to technology in the classroom neglect this type of literacy, stressing technical skills that fail to help students find meaning through a truly educated approach to online reading and writing. Perhaps this explains why such books feel obsolete before the ink dries on their pages. What educators need, therefore, is something more than a discussion of technical issues. To prepare themselves and their students for new types of literacy, they must be receptive to new definitions of the term itself. This requires more than technical knowledge; indeed, it demands that they ask open-ended questions about the human condition, searching for more satisfying definitions and a deeper understanding of these matters.

With this in mind, it may prove helpful to think of literacy in terms of taxonomy. The functional literacy required to read and write letters of an alphabet, and sound the words they form, serves as a stepping stone to more complex types of literacy. By embracing that notion, one invites a more robust definition for literacy's most recent offspring, that troublesome fellow called *computer literacy*. This book encourages definitions that move, purposely stretching literacy to invigorate discussions of computers in education. I shall consider a variety of literacies, all of which come into play when one talks about "literacy in the Digital Age." Some of these terms are familiar; others are heuristics—which means I made them up! Although some may initially strike the reader as odd contrivances, all of these literacies apply to a networked classroom and the online environments in which students increasingly work.

Indeed, just as we must learn to read and write the alphabet to develop functional literacy, so too must we learn how to "read" visual images, discursive practices, personal ethics, community actions, cultural events, global developments, and humanity in general. What's more, while learning to read others online, we are also composing ourselves. This double entendre, which lends itself to the title of this book, suggests the need for composure as well as the desire for invention. We cannot achieve civil discourse online without composure, but neither can we satisfy our need for personal invention without giving full expression to a complex persona, the "saturated selves" that others must interpret through the pastiche of our words and images (Gergen, 1991).

Unfortunately, competence with one form of literacy does not guarantee fluency with another. As a matter of fact, one of the more important questions is whether some forms of literacy are mutually exclusive. Consequently, educators need a far more robust definition for computer literacy, one that takes them well beyond functional literacy. Most schools have passed the stage in which computers are confined to a "keyboarding" or "computer applications" course. Thus, they can no longer view computer literacy in purely technical terms, nor as the province of a particular academic discipline. One's keyboarding skills are hardly a measure of computer literacy at a time when people speak of Netiquette, hypertext narratives, and virtual architecture. For classroom teachers to succeed with the integration of networked technology in preexisting curricula, therefore, they must possess a theoretical foundation as well as technical skills. In fact, the former may prove more significant than the latter, since it will help classroom teachers determine which literacies they value and believe most significant for their students' development.

■ CYBERWRITER AT WORK: THE DESIGN OF THIS BOOK

Obviously, this is not intended as a how-to book, which will, hopefully, spare it the fate of those books gathering dust on the shelves of teachers' lounges and resource centers around the world. I hope that it serves as a philosophical guide while providing practical ideas for classroom practitioners. Toward that end, each chapter begins with a brief discussion of the abstract concerns regarding a particular type of literacy. From the question of definition, I move to discussions of why teachers should be aware of such literacy and the skills students need to acquire it. A series of "literacy challenges," learning activities that encourage critical reading and writing online, will help classroom teachers synthesize theory and practice. In short, I look at ways to use networked technology and online learning environments to teach critical literacy skills. Here's a brief overview of what each chapter has to offer.

Chapter 1, "Media Literacy: Broadening the Definition of Computer Literacy," identifies several shortcomings with impoverished definitions of computer literacy and the pedagogical and curricular approaches they inspire. As a corrective, I propose approaching computer literacy through a more traditional filter: classical rhetoric. By applying rhetoric, the ancient art of persuasion, and the rhetorical triangle of ethos (author's credibility), logos (message's logic), and pathos (emotional appeal to audience), educators will discover important concepts that help students "get outside" themselves and think of "the other"—the writers and audiences they will encounter via electronic mail, newsgroups, chat rooms, Web-based discussion boards, Web sites, and more. Ultimately, this forces a movement away from functional literacy, which has defined computer literacy for much too long, toward a critical literacy that requires far more than technical skills.

Chapter 2, "Civil Literacy: The Cyberpilot's License," emphasizes the fundamental need for students to take responsibility for what they say, how they say it, and the effect it will have on others. This conviction has inspired an online tutorial that provides a forum in which readers may conduct research and continue this discussion. The respective sections of the Web site provide the basis for this chapter, along with relevant literacy challenges. "Know Your Vehicle" presents resources that introduce the history, terms, and technology of the Internet. The "Rights and Responsibilities" section tries to clear the air(waves) and stimulate meaningful discussions. "Who and What Rules the Airwaves" introduces several resources on acceptable-use policies, state and federal laws, and the great debate over freedom of speech on the Internet. In addition, readers may visit the "Reference Desk" to add a link or visit online resources that others have recommended. "Piloting Skills and Netiquette," an interactive primer on the use of electronic mail, search engines, discussion forums, and more, focuses on ethical concerns and definitions of acceptable use.

Chapter 3, "Discourse Literacy: Beyond the Chat Room," assumes familiarity with the concept of civil literacy and a desire to consider online discourse in greater detail. I begin with a distinction between synchronous and asynchronous communication tools, focusing on the former in this chapter. Whether teachers use software such as the Daedalus Integrated Writing Environment, an Internet Relay Chat, or a Web-based message board, they will find ample opportunities to establish healthy discursive practices locally before turning to asynchronous discourse on a national or international level. However, they must be aware that many students have established unhealthy discursive habits during unsupervised, recreational forays into cyberspace. I examine transcripts from classroom sessions, exploring ways to use synchronous, online discussions for instructional purpose. Of particular interest are role-playing activities that enable students to take the position of writers they have studied. This use of pseudonyms presents a singular opportunity for students to adopt the voice and viewpoint of another, stepping outside of themselves as they acquire discourse literacy. The chapter concludes with student evaluations of these exercises, which provide candid insights into this type of learning activity.

Chapter 4, "Personal Literacy: Discovering Oneself Online," reinforces the belief that we must take responsibility for our words and "actions" in an online community. Students need to realize the importance of how they present themselves and how others "read" them. In essence, personal literacy in an online environment compels readers and writers to fashion themselves in words while interpreting the selves they encounter. Teachers need to understand that "praxis doesn't make perfect." Experimentation and reflection are important, but insufficient, if they allow students to practice slovenly habits—from poor grammar to irresponsible flippancy—which frustrates genuine communication and renders students virtually "illiterate" because of their inability to read and write themselves. How might teachers help adolescents hear their own voice and understand how they are "coming across" to others via asynchronous media? I begin with exercises that help students discover what they think, looking at a "Why List" that helps them develop the logos of their arguments before stepping into asynchronous forums where they must use rhetorical strategies to persuade their audience through emotional pathos and a carefully constructed personal ethos. Variations on the "Why List" activity will help individual writers hear their own "voice," question their assumptions, and entertain alternative viewpoints to strengthen their personal literacy.

Chapter 5, "Community Literacy: Composing Ourselves in a Virtual Community," acknowledges the transformation of classroom dynamics through the introduction of networked computer technology. To become an active member of an online community rather than a passive audience, students and teachers must conceive of and conduct their work in new ways. They are no longer reading and writing in the vacuum of an isolated classroom. Instead, their coursework acquires a more authentic quality, engaging with a larger community of learners through telecollaborative endeavors. However, new opportunities also demand new responsibilities, from the "turn taking" in online conversations to careful discretion between public and private messages. The literacy challenges and case studies in this chapter will help students and teachers discuss essential concerns and anticipate potential problems, culminating with the examination of a course Web site as a collaborative work in progress. I'll challenge the misconception that class Web sites are products constructed on completion of a particular project. This requires a look behind the surface of a course Web site that provides interactive writing spaces that serve as communication media as well as an archive of student work. Ultimately, the Web site as a collaborative work in progress is both a creation and reflection of a particular community of learners and an opportunity for students to refine their collaborative skills and community literacy.

Chapter 6, "Visual Literacy: Web Sites, Rhetorically Speaking," builds on the preceding chapter's discussion of a class Web site, particularly the collaborative nature of that undertaking. By helping students understand the process of Web design from the inside out, teachers can demystify the

Web and stimulate critical literacy. To develop their visual literacy, however, students need to understand the rhetorical strategies that Web designers employ. I'll present a case study in which students were asked to read and critique a satirical online article, considering how one can use the rhetoric of Web sites to inspire a critical visual literacy. The reader will gain important insights from an online, synchronous discussion of the satirical article, as well as student reflections on their misreading. This will stimulate questions about how to "read" a Web site with a more critical eye, particularly when the pathos of graphical representations threatens to overwhelm the argument's logos and the writer's ethos. The chapter concludes with guidelines for the rhetorical analysis of Web documents and literacy challenges that ask students to apply visual literacy to the evaluation of hypertexts.

Chapter 7, "Evaluative Literacy: Peer Reviews, Electronic Portfolios, and Online Learning Records," attempts to pull the disparate pieces together. It is often difficult for both students and teachers to keep track of online learning activities. Thus, it is important to reinforce the concept of a writing process, encouraging students to reflect on the road taken to the final product of an essay. Toward that end, I begin with a literacy challenge introducing the concept of a "hypertext writing workshop." Then I examine electronic portfolios and a template that enables students to assemble the respective elements of an essay as a hypertext that includes a topic proposal, process journal, references, rough drafts, and final draft. This approach delivers privileged insights into the composition process, encouraging students to become more competent readers and writers. Finally, the Online Learning Record provides an alternative assessment method that engages the student as part of the evaluation process. The chapter concludes with a brief discussion of the respective sections of the Online Learning Record, which, as an extension of electronic portfolios, is consistent with a process approach to writing. This discussion will inspire teachers who seek alternative approaches to the "grading game" and strategies that help students develop evaluative literacy skills and better judgment of their own process and products.

Chapter 8, "Pedagogical Literacy: Plugging Into Electronic Pedagogy," argues that professional educators must continually refine their ability to "read and write" pedagogical strategies, adapting them to suit their personal styles, curricula, and situations. They must learn how to "think through" emerging technologies, making informed decisions about which tool is most appropriate for a particular group of students and curricular objectives. Some devices are better as "push technology" (e-mail, mailing lists), whereas others require that students "pull" from them (newsgroups, discussion forums, blogs, Web sites). Classroom experience has taught teachers how to integrate texts, chalkboards, overhead projectors, and VCRs—choosing a particular medium based on their knowledge and understanding of what it affords and constrains. They must now develop a similar understanding of new media and the literacies they require and engender. This chapter provides a sense of closure by bringing educators back to the starting point: How do teachers use computer technology to teach literacy skills?

■ HOW TO READ THIS BOOK: A LINEAR APPROACH TO HYPERTEXT

One could approach this book in a hypertextual fashion, starting in the middle and randomly moving forward and backward through the text. However, I'd argue for a more traditional, linear reading. Readers will find that the chapters speak to one another, with earlier ones anticipating their successors, and later ones building on their predecessors' lessons. Thus, each chapter contributes to the book's foundation, simultaneously drawing on earlier points or learning activities while contributing something new to the discussion. Taken as a whole, the book's architecture takes the reader from the overarching theme of computer literacy and the prerequisites of civil literacy to specific literacies that need attention while introducing networked computer technology to a classroom and curriculum.

One type of literacy may concern the reader more than another, but certain fundamental literacies are required before students and teachers attempt complicated online learning activities. For example, the first chapter's discussion of media literacy and the importance of rhetorical traditions establish a framework for the second chapter's concerns with civil literacy. This will, in turn, inform subsequent examination of discourse literacy, community literacy, and global literacy. Meanwhile, some of the concerns of visual literacy overlap with evaluative literacy, but a reversal of their chronology in this text might confuse readers unnecessarily. By gradually shifting from general to specific concerns, the book argues deductively. However, the deliberate movement from personal literacy to community literacy and global literacy describes a trajectory from individual concerns to universal ones. I hope that this will stimulate discussion of local and global currents, simultaneously broadening and deepening our understanding of literacy. I would also hope that it helps a new generation of students learn how to read, write, and interpret their world while composing themselves online.

1

Media Literacy

*Broadening the Definition
of Computer Literacy*

What exactly does it mean to be literate in this world? Well before the 1988 Right to Literacy Conference, which hoped to "address an audience far beyond the bounds of Modern Language Association membership" (Lunsford, Moglen, & Slevin, 1990, p. 1), educators paid a great deal of attention to the empowerment of students through literacy. More than a decade later, however, literacy remains a vexing issue, as illustrated by the keynote address at the 1998 Conference on College Composition and Communication. Cynthia Selfe's (1998) speech was a clarion call for humanists to bring previously neglected matters to the foreground because

> we have a much larger and more complicated obligation to fulfill—
> that of trying to understand and make sense of, to pay attention to,
> how technology is now inextricably linked to literacy and literacy
> education in this country.

When extended, this argument suggests that computer technology's effect on literacy also carries profound implications for the moral education of students, for when it comes to computer literacy, both the rights and responsibilities of those who acquire it must be considered, and teachers must pay attention to far more than the technical skills that would satisfy advocates of an impoverished definition. Just as words enlighten or deceive, serving moral or immoral purposes, so, too, does computer literacy carry potential for good or evil. What is necessary is a more robust definition of this term, one that embraces rhetorical traditions as well as the exploration of human expression through emerging media.

Unfortunately, the repetition of terms such as *computer literacy* in the absence of thoughtful definitions and substantial concern encourages educational institutions to neglect the effect of terminology on students, teachers, and curricula. Contemporary rhetoric reveals an unhealthy pre-occupation with a school's published curriculum and neglect of what Elliot Eisner (1985) describes as the *implicit* and *null curricula*. The implicit curriculum consists of everything a school's personnel teaches through the indirect media of assemblies, dress codes, detentions, and more; the null curriculum refers to neglected subjects, such as auto mechanics, wood-working, and home economics. Often, what educators omit from the school's curriculum or fail to consider as a contributor to the school's ethos is just as important as what they self-consciously include (Eisner, 1985).

It is worth thinking in such terms while examining the effect of the Internet gold rush on schools. To accommodate computer literacy in their K–12 curricula, many schools push to the periphery electives such as music, art, and physical education. This raises two significant questions: As schools introduce computer technology to their classrooms and endorse new expressions of the explicit and implicit curricula, how cognizant are they of their null curriculum's effect on students? While rushing to keep up with technology and placating vocal watchdogs of the explicit curric-ula, are school officials aware of the effect this may have on the implicit curricula?

A fundamental anxiety, which shapes educational curricula more than it should, lurks behind the rhetoric of many computer literacy advocates: "If we don't do something to address this particular ignorance," they argue, "U.S. children will fall behind foreign children and the United States will lose its supremacy." No politician wants to be remembered for allowing the sun to set on the U.S. empire. Nonetheless, myopic defini-tions of terms such as *computer literacy*, and the failure of schools and uni-versities "to make a focused curriculum out of [their] contentiousness," impoverishes educational institutions in ways that few politicians understand (Graff, 1990, p. 825). The end of the 20th Century may well be remembered for the triumph of rhetoric that prompted enormous invest-ments in technology as the panacea for all of public education's malaise. What is most remarkable, however, is how little clarity and substance has accompanied this experiment, which lacks basic definition and philosoph-ical purpose:

> It is often asserted that one of the problems with computers is that too few people know how to use them. The population is accused of being computer illiterate. When calls are made for schools to provide better education in computers, it is not clear what is in mind. (Landauer, 1996, p. 121)

What's more, preoccupation with what a new form of literacy enables may distract one from what it disables. It is naive to think computer liter-acy invites only positive change; implicit in the idea of integration, after all, is a quiet annihilation of that which preceded it. Yet computer literacy advocates seldom acknowledge that one consequence of integrating tech-nology into the classroom is that students will spend more time interact-ing with machines and less time interacting with "unmediated" human beings. Meanwhile, media critics point out that "technologies create the ways in which people perceive reality, and that such ways are the key to understanding diverse forms of social and mental life" (Postman, 1993, p. 21). Thus, introducing the "boxes and wires" of telecomputing into schools is not merely a political or educational issue. It is a moral, philosophical, and cultural issue as well. To proceed with this experiment as if it merely alters a school's explicit curriculum without affecting the implicit and null curricula suggests either a cavalier attitude or epistemological ignorance.

It would be unrealistic to expect classroom teachers to devote equal time and attention to all forms of literacy, so it is wise to ask at this point, as computer literacy gains momentum, what forms of literacy might be marginalized. Seymour Papert (1993), emeritus member of the Epistemology and Learning Group at the Massachusetts Institute of Technology's Media Lab, is representative of those who have little trouble "demoting reading from its privileged position in the school curriculum" because it would liberate children from the "early and massive imposition" of what he calls "letteracy." As Papert (1993) sees it:

> Literacy should not mean the ability to decode strings of alphabetic letters. Consider a child who uses a Knowledge Machine to acquire a broad understanding of poetry (spoken), history (perhaps relived in simulations), and art and science (through computer-based labs), and thus draws on this knowledge to conduct a well-informed, highly persuasive campaign to preserve the environment. All this could happen without being letterate. If it does, should we say the child is illiterate?

Papert (1993) clearly favors a "translation/critical literacy" rather than the traditional "decoding/analytic literacy" taught in public schools (Myers, 1996). Unfortunately, his immersion in computer culture often blinds him to its flaws. Similarly, computer science instructors, preoccupied with the syntax of programming language, seldom pause to consider the "rhetoric of the desktop," or to alert students to the ways in which a computer culture influences their language and perceptions. Nonetheless, students who create "documents" to be saved in "folders" and placed on a "desktop" are learning how to speak a corporate language. How many of them, while acquiring the skills that define computer literacy in myopic technical terms, will have the strength of character to resist the seductions of this metaphor or its effect on their perceptions of the world?

What is particularly disturbing about Papert's (1993) definition of literacy is its indifference toward human relationships with physical environments and peers. In *The Future Does Not Compute*, Stephen Talbott (1995) takes exception with Papert's vision of computer technology as the "primary instrument for overcoming abstraction, reintegrating education with life, and embedding the student in concrete learning situations" (pp. 151–152). Talbott fears a distortion of reality and detachment from humanist concerns, claiming that

> it is a strange definition of "concrete" that places all its stress upon the student's active involvement, and none at all upon whatever it

is he is involved with. The only fully concrete thing a computer offers the student is its own, perhaps enchanting, presence. Beyond that it hosts a mediate and abstract world. . . . This makes it easier for the child to remain caught up in the computer's presentation of reality—and therefore inserts a more distracting, more comprehensive veil between him and the world into which he was born. (p. 152)

■ THE CURRICULAR CONUNDRUM

Given such pernicious possibilities, one may ask why educators should introduce computer-mediated activities to their classrooms. Why should humanities teachers, in particular, take part in shaping computer literacy if it poses a threat to the traditions they value? Such questions were largely absent from the Modern Language Association's Right to Literacy Conference in 1988, where "much of the debate focused on distinctions between functional literacy, cultural literacy, and public literacy" (Costanzo, 1994, p. 11). Yet a decade later, we stretch this attenuated term further by asking it to accommodate emerging technology and electronic texts. Whether the humanities teacher approves or not, "computers are altering the way many of us read, write, and even think. It is not simply that the tools of literacy have changed; the nature of texts, of language, of literacy itself is undergoing crucial transformations" (Costanzo, 1994, p. 11).

Changes in literacy inevitably alter school curricula. Thus, humanists who retreat from the debate over computer literacy in schools may unwittingly invite the end of what they had hoped to preserve: a liberal arts curriculum. What is required, then, is the marriage of emerging technologies with the traditions of rhetorical education, a synthesis that would stimulate school curricula. However, this is not without risks, for the rhetoric and gadgetry of technology have the potential to overwhelm the subtler concerns of a humanities curriculum. One of the most eloquent advocates of such a synthesis is Richard Lanham (1994), who notes that although computer literacy has encouraged an "extraordinary convergence" in university curricula, it also has the potential to displace a central fixture of the humanities curriculum. If allowed, the consequences will extend well beyond schools.

Once you abolish rhetorical education, then you must ask:

How, then, do I teach decorum? What else do I use for my behavioral allegory? Property? Stuff? And what about the teaching of language? Once it has become simply instrumental, the clear, brief, and sincere transmission of neutral fact from one neutral entity to another, it loses . . . its power, as our present literacy crisis attests. If you pursue only clarity, you guarantee obscurity. And people lose their vital interest in language, as any composition teacher can attest. The "literacy crisis" is not only a social crisis, a crisis of instructional leverage, of educational policy, although it is all of those. It comes from the repudiation of the rhetorical heart of Western education, and its linguistic and behavioral education in decorum. (Lanham, 1994, p. 83)

THE RHETORICAL TRIANGLE: ETHOS, ■ LOGOS, AND PATHOS

If the abolition of rhetorical education invites such crises, what exactly can be done to revive "the rhetorical heart of Western education" (Lanham, 1994) while helping students acquire a more satisfying computer literacy? Clearly, this requires a delicate balancing act, merging rhetorical traditions with emerging technologies to arrive at a new synthesis called media literacy (see Figure 1.1).

Figure 1.1

Media Literacy

Media literacy is the ability to read and understand a communications medium by looking *through* the processes it enables, interpreting its signs and symbols, while also looking *at* the medium's effect on an author, audience, and message.

To succeed, we must adopt a holistic approach, establishing a literacy-across-the-curriculum program similar to writing-across-the-curriculum initiatives. Can we ask this of teachers who have not been formally trained in rhetoric? Are teachers of mathematics and science, let alone of the humanities, equipped to pose as rhetoricians? Yes, indeed, for all are engaged in rhetorical activities each day, whether seeking truth or trying to persuade someone to believe a story, cast a vote, buy a product, or take some other action. All of these activities require participation in the ancient art of persuasion that scholars of ancient Greece called rhetoric.

What this shift requires, more than formal training, is a reorientation in the way computers and computer technology are viewed. Until now, we have approved computer literacy as if it were just another form of basic literacy or a functional literacy necessary to succeed in the workplace. These forms of computer literacy required one to "look through" the technology and to learn how to manipulate hardware and software to accomplish certain tasks. However, it is now time to step back from the machinery and look at computers, networks, and the interactions they enable in order to learn how to "read" and interpret their impact. By looking at the machinery instead of constantly looking through it, one returns to the "rhetorical heart" of education while broadening the definition of computer literacy (Haas, 1996; Lanham, 1994).

How to begin? Like this: Return to the foundations of rhetorical analysis, which hold that every message has an author, an argument, and an audience. Rhetoricians speak of these three elements in terms of a "rhetorical triangle" (see Figure 1.2), employing the Greek terms *ethos*, *logos*, and *pathos*, which provide clues to the etymology of modern terms. Ethos speaks to the "ethics" or credibility of the author, logos addresses the "logic" of the message, and pathos relates to the emotional appeal (think of sympathy, empathy, apathy) and how it affects an audience. Whether one speaks of this as ethos, logos, and pathos or author, message, and audience is a matter of personal preference. What is significant, however, is the way this rhetorical approach provides students—and teachers—with a vocabulary and tools for reading and discussing the signs and symbols they encounter both online and off.

Figure 1.2   The Rhetorical Triangle

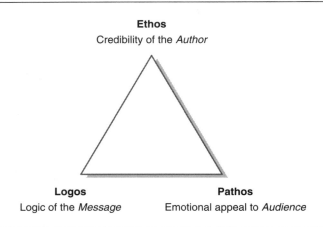

Consider, for instance, television advertising. When a company hires a famous athlete such as Michael Jordan for endorsements, they do so with the knowledge that Jordan's ethos will reflect favorably on their product. Furthermore, by using Jordan's athleticism to create a stunning visual image, accompanied by instrumental music and special effects, the advertisers find their way to the emotional heartbeat of their audience, drawing them in through an effective use of pathos. What is missing? What point on the rhetorical triangle may actually be blunt, compared to the sharp points of ethos and pathos used by this particular medium? In a word: *logos.* Just because Michael Jordan, a tremendously gifted athlete, looks good in a particular pair of athletic shoes, drinks a particular soft drink, or endorses a fast food restaurant does not necessarily mean the product is right for everyone. Indeed, by scratching beneath the surface of these glittering advertisements, teachers can help students see that ethos and pathos are often used to distract the audience from a weak message, one whose logos does not hold up under close examination.

■ MEDIA LITERACY CHALLENGE 1

The Rhetoric of Computer Advertising

One way to help students develop media literacy skills is by asking them to apply rhetorical analysis to another kind of advertising.

What to Do

1. To initiate this challenge, ask students to find an advertisement for computer hardware, software, or accessories in a popular magazine. Have them examine the ethos, logos, and pathos used to sell the product to that magazine's intended audience.

2. Ask students to bring the advertisement and analysis to class. Have them form small groups, share the advertisements, and see if they can guess what type of magazine published them. Each group should list common images, themes, and methods used to express logos, establish ethos, and appeal through pathos.

3. In a subsequent discussion with the full group, create a list of rhetorical strategies that computer manufacturers use to persuade people that their product is truly the best and that a customer should act immediately by purchasing that product.

IS EVERYTHING AN ARGUMENT?   ■

Placing rhetoric at the heart of computer literacy not only broadens the definition of the latter term but also helps students cultivate critical literacy while engaged in recreational computer use. Consider, for example, the habit of browsing, or "surfing," the Internet, which has quickly become a diversion comparable to channel surfing television programs. What is often missing from these activities is the kind of critical thinking teachers would like to instill in their students. Unless they are encouraged to think critically, students may simply acquire meaningless information that they fail to scrutinize or document in research papers.

This leads to an ethos problem. The student who borrows intellectual property without proper citations or uses inaccurate information gathered from a dubious source inevitably loses credibility. In such instances, the rhetorical triangle reminds students to consider all three fundamental concerns—ethos, logos, and pathos—before rushing to judgment. As a result, the rhetorical triangle furnishes a powerful means for analysis and articulation, serving as both an instrument of inquiry and a vocabulary for expression. Students who randomly pluck information from the Internet may not realize they have fallen prey to the salesmanship of pathos, which disarms their critical judgment by appealing to their emotions, distracts them with faulty logos, and leads them into the temptations that damage their ethos.

One may teach this lesson through the rhetorical strategies of daily life, since their prevalence alone helps students realize the importance of interpreting signs and symbols to develop media literacy skills. To emphasize a point, as well as start an argument, some rhetoricians claim "everything's an argument" (Lunsford & Ruszkiewicz, 1999). Although an overstatement, this is certainly a good starting point for discussion. While there is evidence of ethos, logos, and pathos in every statement read, seen, or heard, not all statements make the same kind of argument. Granted, this is not the kind of argument that adolescents have with their siblings, nor is it necessarily one in which the participants attempt to win a debate.

Rather, it is the kind of argument that comes from either (a) attempting to discover truth or (b) after having discovered that truth, attempting to persuade others to take an action (Lunsford & Ruszkiewicz, 1999, p. 5).

When seen through this filter, a surprising number of statements—written, visual, musical, and virtual—acquire an argumentative quality. In other words, they can be viewed as rhetorical devices that attempt to persuade a particular audience. They may wish to share a truth, telling the audience that "Not marble, nor the gilded monuments/Of Princes, shall outlive this pow'rful rhyme" (Shakespeare, 1964, p. 95); then again, they may wish to stir the audience to take action, submitting to the power of the statements' persuasion.

■ MEDIA LITERACY CHALLENGE 2

Arguments "R" Us

This challenge helps sensitize students to a wide range of arguments they encounter on a daily basis.

What to Do

1. Divide the class into small groups and ask each group to consider one of the following questions:

   (1) Is a love letter an argument?

   (2) Is a grocery list an argument?

   (3) Is a restaurant's menu an argument?

   (4) Is a vacation itinerary an argument?

   (5) Is a birthday party invitation an argument?

   (6) Is a course syllabus an argument?

   (7) Is a standardized examination an argument?

   (8) Is a report card an argument?

   (9) Is a computer program an argument?

   (10) Is a Web site an argument?

Teacher's Tip

Although all of the items could be seen as arguments, students may have difficulty understanding this concept initially. Nonetheless, when they have begun to see their world through rhetorical filters, they should be ready to look at computer paraphernalia in new ways, subjecting it to similar critiques.

---

2. Ask students how each item might present an argument and what media are used to express it. How do those media use ethos, logos, and pathos to convince an audience that their message is true or persuade them to take action?

Expanding the Challenge

To further develop students' understanding of rhetorical filters, ask them to write a brief rhetorical analysis of the promotional copy used in the packaging of computer merchandise. What evidence is there that the manufacturers have employed ethos, logos, and pathos to persuade the user that this is a quality product?

Suggested topics: The cover, table of contents, and blurb of a CD-ROM, computer manual, or software application. Help students discover distinctions between advertisements for computer merchandise in various media and the promotional material found on the merchandise itself.

Questions for discussion: How are the imagery and text on the merchandise different from the imagery seen in the magazine ads? Is there a difference, or do they "echo" the persuasive tactics used in advertising campaigns?

THE TECHNOLOGY OF WRITING   ■

Ultimately, computer literacy needs to be considered as part of a larger discussion and placed in the context of significant cultural, historical, and technological developments. Just as typewriting classes gave way to keyboarding classes, computer application courses that isolate various software applications and treat the computer primarily in technical terms may also disappear. Until that happens, however, educators need to make a concentrated effort to situate computer literacy in the larger context of media literacy. This serves a number of purposes while calling attention to frequently neglected concerns. For instance, despite the attention that the Internet and computer technology have attracted, how often do people actually think about the impact of writing technology on their writing and thinking?

In his book, *Writing Space: The Computer, Hypertext, and the History of Writing*, Jay David Bolter (1991) describes writing as "a state of mind" while arguing for broader definitions of fundamental terms. In fact, Bolter not only argues that pencils, pens, paper, and computers are writing technology, but also that the skills themselves are technological inventions:

> There is good etymological reason to broaden our definition of technology to include skills as well as machines. The Greek root of "technology" is techne, and for the Greeks a techne could be an art or a craft, "a set of rules, system or method of making or doing, whether of the useful arts, or of the fine arts" (Liddell & Scott, 1973, p. 1785). . . . In the ancient world, physical technology was simpler, and the ancients put a correspondingly greater emphasis on the skill of the craftsman—the potter, the stone-mason, or the carpenter. In his dialogue the Phaedrus, Plato calls the alphabet itself a techne. He would also have called the ancient book composed of ink on papyrus a techne; Homeric epic poetry was also a techne, as was Greek tragedy. All the ancient arts and crafts have this in common: that the craftsman must develop a skill, a technical state of mind in using tools and materials. Ancient and modern writing is a technology in just this sense. It is a method for arranging verbal thoughts in a visual space. The writer always needs a surface upon which to make his or her marks and a tool with which to make them, and these materials help to define the nature of the writing. Writing with quill and parchment is a different skill from writing with a printing press, which in turn differs from writing with a computer. (p. 35)

■ MEDIA LITERACY CHALLENGE 3

Musical Chairs and Writing Technology

This challenge will transform writing technology by turning what is usually invisible and common into something visible and extraordinary. In doing so, it raises questions to inspire further exploration of writing technology as well as classroom discussions about media literacy. As a result, this literacy challenge illustrates the need for broader definitions and a deeper understanding of the technology and media that students employ while developing literacy skills.

What to Do

1. Divide the class into groups of three or four students.

2. Ask each group to spend 5 minutes brainstorming a story idea about "a person in a place with a problem."

3. After they have established their outline, each group begins at one of seven workstations, each of which presents a different writing technology. By way of illustration, the workstations for this exercise could provide:

   Station 1: Chalk and chalkboard.

   Station 2: Crayon or charcoal and large, unlined poster paper.

   Station 3: Pencil and unlined paper.

   Station 4: Pen and lined paper.

   Station 5: Markers and a whiteboard.

   Station 6: Manual typewriter and typing paper with correction fluid.

   Station 7: Laptop or desktop computer and diskette.

   If any of these materials are unavailable, use comparable substitutes to approximate the evolution of writing technology from its simplest to most complex forms. Groups have 5 minutes to work on their story's narrative, using the writing technology at the station. Instrumental music provides a soothing background as well as practical purpose: When the music stops, so must the composition. Each group member must contribute at least one sentence to the narrative using the designated writing technology to write the sentence.

4. As soon as the music stops, each group steps back from its workstation and leaves its final sentence in a state of arrested development.

5. The groups rotate, moving to the next station in the sequence, where they read and continue their predecessors' narrative—beginning with that incomplete sentence—while using the new writing technology before them.

6. After the groups have completed a full rotation of the stations, so that everyone has had an opportunity to use each of the writing technologies, ask students to complete the survey form in Figure 1.3.

Figure 1.3

Media Literacy: Informal Study of Writing Technology

Name: _____

For each of the following, please use the space provided or write a brief commentary on the back of this sheet.

1. Which writing technology felt most comfortable? Briefly explain why you liked the "feel" of this combination most. Put another way, which combination allowed you to concentrate most on the narrative you were writing?

   ___ Chalk and chalkboard

   ___ Crayon on large, unlined poster paper

   ___ Pencil and unlined paper

   ___ Pen and lined paper

   ___ Markers on a whiteboard

   ___ Manual typewriter and typing paper

   ___ Laptop or desktop computer

2. Which combination called the most attention to itself, distracting you from the narrative, and how did it do this?

3. How did the respective writing spaces affect your sentence length or style? (In other words, how concerned were you with trying to fit your words and sentences into that writing space?)

4. If you had a choice of writing implement and writing space—that is, the tool and the surface on which it is used—which would you choose for the following activities, and why?

   Grocery list:

   Love letter:

   Diagram/map:

   Academic essay:

   A reminder (to yourself or family member):

5. Of these technologies, which do you think would be most useful to the writer who wished to emphasize the following, and why?

   —Ethos (the author's credibility)

   —Logos (the message)

   —Pathos (emotional appeal to the audience)

■ CIVIL LITERACY

Teacher's Tip

When students have completed this survey, consider having them discuss it in their original small groups or in new groupings. Alternatively, it might be worthwhile to facilitate a full-class discussion on "Writing Technology: Evolution or Revolution?" If addressed as an open-ended question, this question helps students think about computers and computer literacy as both an evolutionary and revolutionary process. As a result, they should begin to see computer literacy in a new light, discussing it as part of a historical movement situated in the larger context of media literacy.

Once teachers have widened the parameters of computer literacy, enabling students to think of it in terms of media literacy, it is time to examine less technical matters. As already shown, there is far more to online learning environments than the "boxes and wires" that enable telecomputing. In many ways, the assembly of hardware and software presents fewer challenges than the creation of an online community of learners, particularly if the participants fail to behave in a manner conducive to educational endeavors. Having considered ways to restore the rhetorical heart of education to computer literacy, however, teachers are better prepared to cultivate civil literacy in cyberspace.

2

Civil Literacy

The Cyberpilot's License

Approaching computer literacy as a form of media literacy may help restore "the rhetorical heart of Western education" (Lanham, 1994), but to fulfill that ambition, educators must help students consider the moral and ethical issues that accompany their use of technology. This calls for a more enlightened approach to networked technology, one that realizes its potential to do both good and evil in schools and communities. Although this technology can be used to create a sense of community online, it can also be used to exclude or marginalize individuals and misappropriate intellectual property. At present, most school districts require that students and their guardians sign an Acceptable-Use Policy (AUP) before granting Internet access to pupils. However, this proves to be a legalistic measure rather than an educational one. As an antidote, this chapter proposes a more thoughtful approach to what is commonly called "Netiquette." This approach requires an essential literacy for children whose education introduces them to powerful, technological tools: civil literacy (see Figure 2.1).

Figure 2.1

> ### Civil Literacy
>
> Civil literacy is the ability to read, interpret, and respect the moral and ethical beliefs embraced by a particular social group and apply them in a responsible manner.

In December 1994, one of the earliest guidelines for AUPs appeared on the Internet, advising policymakers to "make it clear that use of the Net is a privilege and not a right, and outline the penalties and repercussions of violating the AUP" (Classroom Connect, 1994). Indeed, many school districts followed this advice, initiating students to the Web not through an educational program but through a legal document full of oblique warnings and ambiguous threats. Why is this such a pernicious development? If one thinks of an AUP as part of a school's implicit curriculum, then these documents could make schools less conducive to intelligent educational practice and less hospitable to the children they were designed to protect. This ought to make one ask a few troublesome questions. For example: Is an AUP designed to protect children from pornography on the Internet or to defend schools from civil suits? Ultimately, whom does the AUP serve? Whom does it protect?

Defendants of these litigious documents speak in fatalistic terms when they ask, "How else can we protect children and establish the rules?" This, however, exposes the flawed thinking, and disingenuous character, of an AUP. A school that distributes such documents without an introductory course to accompany them is more concerned with legal issues than education. What's more, these AUPs reveal an unhealthy preoccupation with a school's published curriculum and neglect the implicit and null curricula that influence children.

■ THE CYBERPILOT'S LICENSE

Draconian threats have seldom taught students how to drive cars or prevent unwanted pregnancies. Certainly, educators need to offer children guidance for telecomputing as well as other activities, but AUPs, as presently conceived, are legalistic and threatening when they ought to be instructive. As a corrective measure, faculty representatives from all disciplines ought to develop a program that addresses the concerns that accompany computer literacy, teaching what is meant by the responsible use of computer technology. This proposal should not be confused with a number of commercial ventures promoting an "Internet driver's license," which stresses technical skills. Instead, I would propose a cyberpilot's license to focus on the civil literacy that must accompany technical skills so students give more thought to the moral and ethical issues raised by networked technology. AUPs are a component, although not necessarily the centerpiece, of such a program, just as driver's education is a requirement for anyone who wishes to obtain permission to operate an automobile on public roadways. Meanwhile, readers primarily interested in devising a computer literacy course that stresses functional literacy would do well to visit the Web site for the European Computer Driving License (http://www.ecdl.com/). Established by a nonprofit organization in Ireland, this program offers a complete syllabus featuring seven learning modules and a scope and sequence designed to create international standards.

Critics of this proposal may consider it an unnecessary encroachment on academic curricula. Others will quarrel over the appropriate place for it in the curriculum. Both responses, however, produce the kind of myopic and evasive stances that perpetuate the "overly-narrow, official version of literacy practices or skills" that Selfe (1998) has admonished language arts educators to resist. Educators cannot dismiss Netiquette as irrelevant, banishing it to the null curriculum, nor can they allow disputes over its proper place in the curriculum to stall its introduction. Traditionally, few computer science courses have given "Web ethics" more than a peripheral glance. Meanwhile, humanities teachers complain they already have too much to do and too little expertise with telecomputing to accept such responsibilities. However, emerging technologies blur the distinctions between disciplines, compelling simultaneous instruction of skills and the responsibility inherent in their exercise. "Computer ethics" must, therefore, be an integral part of any class that uses computers—and a prerequisite for computer literacy.

KNOW YOUR VEHICLE ■

Despite a century's experience with automobiles, a significant number of drivers still operate a vehicle without understanding its mechanics, nor do they believe it necessary to acquire such understanding. Although this may be true, it betrays an alarming and willful ignorance that merits a qualifier. Such ignorance may not prevent one from operating a vehicle, but it could eventually lead to significant problems. Failure to understand why an automobile engine needs clean engine oil, a functional radiator with coolant, or balanced tires and proper alignment may not prevent one from driving a vehicle (for a while). However, it's just a matter of time before something breaks down, forcing the operator to consult someone who does understand the vehicle. The same applies to networked computers and the "cyberpilots" who use them to navigate through cyberspace. What one doesn't know may not prevent one from making these vehicles work, but it could ultimately do harm.

Students may protest that studying the history, terminology, and technology of the Internet is boring or unnecessary, but teachers should explain that one cannot achieve computer literacy without the knowledge necessary to place all of this in a larger social and cultural context. As with driver education, networked computers present opportunities that did not previously exist. They have, however, evolved out of traditions that adolescents cannot fully appreciate without greater historical perspective. Thus, it helps to know a little about the history of the Internet, as provided by a resource like Hobbes' Internet Timeline (http://www.zakon.org/robert/internet/timeline/), or to have knowledge of a glossary of Internet terms, like the primer from the Internet Literacy Consultants (http://www.matisse.net/files/glossary.html). A brief introduction to the history and terminology helps students see that although cyberspace offers new possibilities, many of the activities they encounter there have historical antecedents. Also, familiarity with the terminology is an integral part of literacy and is critical to the kind of civility educators wish to inspire. Before students reach for the slang terms used to describe online activities, it is worthwhile to identify the formal terms that help define the language of this culture.

Background knowledge of this sort proves useful when students turn to primers that will help them understand how the Internet works and how they can harness its power for educational purposes. There are many online tutorials to choose from, including the multilingual introduction, Learn the Net (http://www.learnthenet.com/english/index.html), and a basic introduction for beginners, Internet 101 (http://internet101.org). Services and Web sites like these present a veritable encyclopedia of resources for learning and teaching Internet skills, including a wealth of hyperlinks to carefully selected resources and thoughtful annotations that include brief reviews. With such an embarrassment of riches to choose from, teachers might wish to arrange a scavenger hunt for students to find the best online primer. However, it helps to establish criteria first, so that an online search doesn't deteriorate into casual browsing or random selection of mediocre or misleading resources.

As students gain familiarity with the "vehicle," they may want to know more about All Search Engines (http://www.allsearchengines.com), listservs, newsgroups, and more. And what of the students who come to class with a fairly good understanding of the vehicle? If they already know the vehicle, should they take part in exercises such as this? Absolutely! In fact, they should be deputized to assist their teacher and classmates. This is a good opportunity to model a collaborative approach to learning, which sits at the core of civil literacy.

■ RIGHTS AND RESPONSIBILITIES

As mentioned earlier, the flaws in AUPs for technology stem from a preoccupation with legal concerns rather than educational ones. As a result, these policy statements typically focus on the rules and regulations that govern student behaviors and the consequences for disobeying them. What's missing from this equation? How about an understanding of why these rules and regulations exist? Imagine approaching student questions as an educational opportunity rather than a disciplinary threat. Perhaps what adults interpret as sarcasm or insolence actually reveals relative inexperience ("Why can't we use each other's personal accounts?"), fundamental ignorance ("Why should we refrain from flame wars?"), or a First Amendment challenge ("Why can't we view pornography in school if it's protected as free speech?").

Schools often rely on threats, like those featured in the AUP, to force student compliance, rather than appealing to the better part of human nature. As a consequence, schools neglect or inhibit a child's natural curiosity, which often expresses itself through a desire to understand why certain actions and activities are prohibited. To repair some of the damage done to their students' intellectual curiosity, teachers may wish to have them visit the Center for Democracy and Technology (http://www.cdt.org), a nonprofit organization that develops and advocates for public policies that support constitutional civil liberties and democratic values in new computer and communications technologies. Students would also benefit from learning about the Computer Professionals for Social Responsibility (CPSR, http://www.cpsr.org/), a group that seeks to raise awareness of the forces involved in the development of cyberspace while promoting civil liberties through the CPSR Cyber-Rights (http://www.cpsr.org/prevsite/cpsr/nii/cyberrights). This could, in fact, inspire discussions about distinctions between privileges and rights; a student's computer privileges may be revoked, but what about his or her civil liberties?

WHO AND WHAT RULES THE AIRWAVES? ■

It seldom hurts to understand the context within which an individual operates. Therefore, this section of "The Cyberpilot's License" addresses a quintessential problem of the human condition: How can a part survey the whole? The Internet is a vast, collaborative work in progress. As such, it may seem as though no one is in charge of it. That may have been true once, but as more people have gone online and as celebrated cases have called attention to the need for rules and regulations, a whole new genre of legislation has arrived. To reach an understanding of AUPs, state and federal laws, and the great debate over freedom of speech on the Internet, one must investigate civil literacy in cyberspace. Students and teachers can also locate definitions of important terms, laws, and cases concerning censorship on the Internet, as well as various opinions on the question, by visiting Ohio University's Free Speech Web page (http://www.ohiou .edu/esl/project/freespeech/index.html).

PILOTING SKILLS AND NETIQUETTE ■

By now, it should be obvious that there's far more to civil literacy than technical skills. However, teachers seeking concrete exercises that "show" what the previous sections "tell" will find what they are looking for here in "Piloting Skills and Netiquette." This section introduces students to several problematic issues they will encounter while flying through the information skyway. Hopefully, by the time they have completed these exercises, they will never again think of computer literacy as a purely technical skill, nor will they suffer the delusion that online activities can be divorced from social and cultural concerns.

   Print limitations do not permit a full sampling of the learning activities available in this section of "The Cyberpilot's License." For now, this limited sampling should reinforce the significance of civil literacy in cyberspace, stimulating class discussions while providing a glimpse of learning activities that facilitate further inquiry. The following, abbreviated versions will enable classroom teachers to review learning activities without sitting in front of a computer screen. Later chapters will present further selections, but this section begins with two fundamental concerns of civil literacy in cyberspace: intellectual property and human rights.

INTELLECTUAL PROPERTY ■
IN CYBERSPACE: AN OVERVIEW

One of the most important distinctions for a scholar, both online and off, is the difference between referencing information and stealing it. This applies not only to the physical world, but also to the intellectual one. Unless students understand this distinction, they may harm others or themselves in cyberspace. This overview should help cyberpilots in training gain respect for what is known as intellectual property. It introduces general principles and specific guidelines for refraining from the misuse or abuse of intellectual property. The entire exercise is, in fact, guided by the notion that safe cyberpilots learn how to borrow without stealing.

Private E-mail

Private e-mail is, first and foremost, private material. Before one considers using a quotation from private e-mail, be sure to ask permission from the author. If the individual isn't comfortable with another's use of the message, then the writer is ethically bound to omit that document from his or her essay. However, if the author does grant permission, the document must be cited properly. Here's why and how to do that.

Why

Tell students to resist the temptation to simply cut and paste a passage from e-mail into an essay. Why? Because the ideas, and their expression, belong to someone else. Respect other people's property, whether it's intellectual or physical. Also, writers could find themselves in very deep trouble if the individual from whom they are borrowing this passage should decide to use the exact same one in the report he or she is writing for the same class. So, give credit where credit is due: Document that e-mail message! Otherwise, writers risk damaging their ethos, which means their credibility and reputation will suffer.

How

There is still debate over the issue of how to cite electronic sources, so if something seems odd to you, investigate the Web or printed handbooks to see if better alternatives have emerged. For the sake of consistency, let's adopt the Modern Language Association (MLA) guidelines for citing electronic sources. The MLA would cite itself as follows:

> Gibaldi, Joseph. *MLA Handbook for Writers of Research Papers*. New York: Modern Languages Association of America. 2003.

Depending on the academic discipline and the teacher's preferences, writers may wish to use a different reference style, such as the American Psychological Association guidelines or the *Chicago Manual of Style*. What matters most is consistency, so choose one set of guidelines or another, but make certain to stress the need to provide complete bibliographical references. For further information on bibliographical information, consult a handbook or visit a reputable online source such as the Internet Public Library's archives for citing electronic resources (http://www.ipl.org/div/farq/netciteFARQ.html). For now, here is what the *MLA Handbook* suggests for citing electronic mail messages:

> Give the name of the writer; the title of the message (if any), taken from the subject line and enclosed in quotation marks; a description of the message that includes the recipient (e.g. "E-mail to the author); and the date of the message. (Gibaldi, 1999, p. 199)

For example, let's say that Penelope Jones received an e-mail message from Josephine Smith. The subject line of the message was "Yikes, how do

I do this?" Penelope received it on April 1, 2003. If Penelope wanted to use this item in an essay, how would she cite it? According to the MLA conventions, the bibliographical citation would look like this:

> Smith, Josephine. "Yikes, how do I do this?" E-mail to Penelope Jones. 1 April 2003.

Mailing List Messages

What is a "mailing list" (or listserv), anyway? Think of it as a public forum that distributes messages through an "electronic mailbox in the sky." People from all over the world subscribe to this mailbox so that whenever someone puts a message in it, they, along with all other subscribers, automatically receive a copy of that message. So, unlike "snail mail" or even faxes, messages sent to a listserv allow for "one-to-many" correspondence without the writer sending more than one copy through the airwaves.

Cyberpilots are sometimes tempted to borrow ideas or information from interesting messages encountered on electronic mailing lists, as though these items are free for the taking because they appear in a public forum. This is an unethical practice, however, and one that must be avoided. Here's why.

Why

Building a community of learners is like building a house: Both need a solid foundation. The foundation for the community of learners is personal integrity. If cyberpilots steal ideas and information from strangers they have encountered on electronic mailing lists, without noting the source, can you imagine the difficulty future scholars will have in trying to locate the origins of this information? Do not borrow material from mailing lists without citing it properly. On the spur of the moment, this may save time, but in the long run, it could damage reputations, spoil integrity, and confuse individuals who rely on a community of scholars to assist their research.

How

The MLA guidelines offer the following advice:

> To cite a posting to an e-mail discussion list, begin with the author's name and the title of the document (in quotation marks), as given in the subject line, followed by the description Online posting, the date when the material was posted, the name of the forum . . . , the date of access and, in angle brackets, the online address of the list's Internet site or, if no Internet site is known, the e-mail address of the list's moderator or supervisor. (Gibaldi, 1999, p. 200)

So, imagine this: A student named Nicky Murrieta posted a message entitled "Communication in Cyberspace" to a listserv for a project called "The Media Matter" on September 2, 2003. You have this e-mail message because you were subscribed to the project mailing list (mediamatter@ jaring.my) and received the message on September 3, 2003. The project had no Web site then, nor does it have one now, but the moderator's e-mail address was buddyb@iskl.po.my. What to do? Try this:

Murrieta, Nicky. "Communication in Cyberspace." Online posting. 2 September 2003. The Media Matter. 3 September 1999. (buddyb@iskl.po.my).

Newsgroup Messages

What is a "newsgroup," and how would you know one when you saw it? Well, perhaps it would help to think of newsgroups as discussion groups or message boards arranged by theme, with technology keeping the "minutes" of their conversations. There are literally thousands of newsgroups on virtually every topic one can imagine. Before the World Wide Web made it possible to access information through Web sites with graphic images, "Usenet newsgroups" were one of the most popular ways of sharing information online. They are still quite popular, perhaps because, unlike a mailing list, a user doesn't need to subscribe to a newsgroup. The user goes to it, rather than having its messages automatically come to the user. In time, one is grateful for this!

All newsgroups are not necessarily about news. Rather, they bring together people interested in a particular topic, ranging from politics to recreation, activism to alternative lifestyles. In these groups, one might hear eyewitness accounts of social protests, natural disasters, and other historic events. One can also join discussions about film, music, sports, and other recreation. To learn more about the possibilities, visit the Google Groups archive (http://groups.google.com/). However, before flying into a particular newsgroup, cyberpilots should make sure they know what they are getting into. Upon arrival at a newsgroup forum, it's often wise to "lurk before you leap" into a discussion, getting oriented in the conversation by first making certain this is the right place. If it's not, then exit and check out another newsgroup. You are bound to find one of interest, because there are tens of thousands, but finding a niche may seem rather intimidating at first.

After finding the right newsgroup, it is still important to remember the context of the conversation and always consider sources. Before snatching an interesting quote from a newsgroup, one needs to learn something about the individual who made the statement, especially if he or she presents obscure facts that need verification. Good scholarship depends largely on good, reliable sources of information. So before using a newsgroup message in an essay, it's a good idea to do a little homework on the source itself.

Why

As with messages from a mailing list, it's essential that one gives credit where credit is due, providing a source that other scholars can locate. This demonstrates that one has done the necessary homework instead of shooting from the hip, tossing words and ideas around carelessly.

How

According to the MLA, here's how to handle newsgroup sources:

To cite a posting to a Usenet news group, begin with the author's name and the title of the document (in quotation marks), as given in the subject line, followed by the description Online posting, the date when the material was posted, the date of access, and, in angle brackets, the name of the newsgroup with the prefix news. (Gibaldi, 1999, p. 201)

For example: Imagine that someone named I. M. Patriotic posted a message entitled "Big Bend Is Awesome!" on the "National Parks" newsgroup (rec.outdoors.national-parks) on July 4, 2003. Because newsgroup messages are automatically archived, a student might discover this posting on October 31, 2004. Following MLA guidelines, the citation would look like this:

Patriotic, I. M. "Big Bend Is Awesome!" Online posting. 4 July 2003. 31 October 2004. (news: rec.outdoors.national-parks).

Synchronous Communication (Multiuser Domains, Internet Relay Chats)

"Context is everything," they say, for a writer must always bear in mind the situation from which a comment is taken. Quotes taken out of context are often misleading, delivering either a half-truth or a complete distortion. This is especially true when it comes to synchronous online communications. In these conversations, the speakers are individuals typing at their own keyboards, often separated by distance, yet connected through the Internet in a conversation that materializes on their respective screens at nearly the same moment. Before using material from such conversations in an essay or report, it is absolutely critical that one consider the context of the remarks, then make sure to properly acknowledge the author of those remarks.

Why

As with private e-mail, the author of the message may not be comfortable with its use in another medium. Secure permission before using quotations. If permission is denied, look for other sources of information. If permission is granted, be sure to give full credit and provide sufficient information to allow the reader of the essay to understand the context of these remarks. If not, the work will lack credibility, and the report will sound more like gossip than research. Students need to be careful because their reputation is at stake as well as their relationship with the individual they chose to quote. Also, their ethos, the credibility that they need to persuade an audience, suffers whenever they cut corners or employ unreliable sources of information. Chat rooms may be entertaining, but one should never select material from them without first considering the source, the context, and its appropriateness in a scholarly work.

How

There are a number of ways synchronous conversations take place online. However, the MLA guidelines seem broad enough to encompass most variations in this genre. Here's what they have to say:

> To cite a synchronous communication posted in a forum such as a MUD (multiuser domain), or MOO (multiuser domain, object-oriented), give the name of the speaker (if you are citing just one), a description of the event, the date of the event, the forum for the communication (e.g., LinguaMOO), the date of access, and the network address, with the prefix telnet://. (Gibaldi, 1999, p. 201)

It's worth noting that the MLA encourages writers to provide "an archival version of the communication" whenever possible (Gibaldi, 1999, p. 202), but it is often not possible. Also, in order to provide a context for the discussion, a writer may wish to cite more than one speaker. So, let's imagine that a student wants to cite a conversation between two speakers, Justin Brownie and Kiki Buttafucco, involved in a MOO session discussing the merits of synchronous writing environments for educational purposes. The discussion took place in Cheshire MOOn, a MOO maintained at the University of Texas, as part of an interactive panel discussion entitled "Can You MOO?" during a conference held on January 31, 2000. If the student discovered a transcript of this discussion on April 20, 2000, the citation would look like this:

> Brownie, Justin and Kiki Buttafucco. Conference panel. "Can You MOO?" 31 January 2000. CheshireMOOn. 20 April 2000. (telnet://cheshire.cwrl.utexas.edu:7777)

World Wide Web Message Board Entries

A "discussion forum" (or "message board") is a place in a Web site where one finds asynchronous conversation (conversations between people who are not online at the same time). Similar to newsgroups, a discussion forum may be dedicated to a particular topic; unlike many newsgroups, however, discussion forums are usually situated in the context of a Web site. For example, a Web site for a professional football team might include a discussion forum where fans gather to discuss the team's performance. Thus, the information one finds in a discussion forum is the collection of messages produced by cyberpilots with a common interest. If a student should "borrow" information from a Web-based discussion forum, he or she would need to cite its location on the Web.

Why

Inexperienced cyberpilots make the mistake of thinking "no one will notice if I borrow just one quote from a discussion forum." However, the moment writers steal intellectual property and introduce it into an essay or report, presenting it as if it is their own, they have compromised their integrity. If the idea or information that is stolen proves especially interesting and others wish to learn more about it, how does one direct them to its source? By failing to keep track of sources, and committing plagiarism by stealing thoughts from discussion forums, a writer will do considerable damage to the community of learners who depend on each other.

How

Here's what the MLA advises:

Begin with the author's name and the title of the posting (if there is one), in quotation marks, followed by the description Online posting, the date when the material was posted, the name of the forum, the date of access, and, in angle brackets, the network address. (Gibaldi, 1999, pp. 200–201)

Web Sites and Databases

All of the electronic resources considered thus far have come from rather informal sources. Indeed, it is their informality that leads some students to think excerpts can be "borrowed" without formal citation. Clearly, this leads to problems, particularly when more than one student uses the same quotation from an e-mail message, discussion forum, newsgroup, mailing list, or synchronous chat. The same is true for information "borrowed" from Web sites that do not present the name of a specific author. The temptation to take intellectual property from these sources without proper attribution is strong, but unless students resist that temptation, they will contribute to a breakdown of the rules that bind and maintain a community of learners. Before leaving this discussion, therefore, it is important to consider some of the formal publications encountered on the World Wide Web.

Chapter 6, "Visual Literacy," looks more closely at Web sites and how to subject them to a critical reading. For the time being, though, the reader needs to distinguish between Web documents (everything from articles and essays to film clips and sound bites), Web pages (individual pages of a site), and the Web sites themselves (the sum of all these parts). An entire chapter of this book could be dedicated to the proper citation for various Web documents; however, what is most important is to establish the basics that students can apply to a wide range of Web resources. They will quickly note parallels between the citations for print and electronic books, essays, and articles. However, what they may overlook is the need to cite photographs, illustrations, song lyrics, and other documents they find on the Web. In all cases, students should secure permission for using these items before integrating them into their work. Citations alone are not sufficient. When in doubt, it's best to ask for permission and footnote that source, and that brings up the matter of the source itself.

Before writers snatch something from the World Wide Web, it is essential that they determine the source of that information and whether its creators would want them to borrow it. Just because it is technically possible to do something, one shouldn't assume it's a moral, legal, or ethical practice. This is where the analogy between physical and intellectual property is important for developing civil literacy in cyberspace. Many students use the "copy/paste" functions on their keyboard to import documents without subjecting them to close scrutiny first. (This is the equivalent of photocopying articles from microfilm and microfiche in the library without first checking to see if the article will be useful.) It's important to understand the distinction between Web sites, Web pages, and Web documents. After students understand that everything on a Web page within a Web site should be considered a document created by another person, they will be more sensitive to the concerns of intellectual property. It's in their best interest, after all, because most consumers of information on the Web eventually become creators of intellectual property themselves. "What goes around, comes around," and in this case, that makes civil literacy a necessity. Students must, therefore, learn to place a Web document in its proper context, determining who is the owner of that property.

For starters, students should learn how to read the "uniform resource locator" (URL), or Web address, for a site. Let's take a look at one. The Computer Writing and Research Lab at the University of Texas has the following URL: http://www.cwrl.utexas.edu. What does each part mean? Here's a breakdown (with parenthetical explanations):

> http—hypertext transfer protocol (the "language" computers use to transfer Web documents)
>
> www—World Wide Web (the medium in which we're working)
>
> cwrl—Computer Writing and Research Lab (the computer server that holds Web documents)
>
> utexas—University of Texas's domain name (the larger organization within which the writing and research lab resides)
>
> edu—educational (the "domain suffix" or classification of this organization)

Perhaps the first thing for students to look at is the final item in the URL. The domain gives the first clue, providing an institutional context. If ".edu" appears in the address, the site was created at an educational institution. The documents one finds there might be free for the taking, but they most definitely require proper citations and, in many cases, permission. Similar rules apply to documents found on government Web sites, which typically feature ".gov" at the end of their address. Commercial sites, which end with the suffix ".com," might not allow access to documents without payment. Even then, however, a writer ought to provide full and proper citations. Whether .edu, .gov, or .com, as always, it is important to know the source of information before relying too heavily on it in research. Otherwise, one could mistake propaganda for objective information.

Why

Web documents did not fall from the sky, nor were they created for cyberpilots to pillage. One must respect intellectual property, giving full and proper reference to the authors, organizations, and Web sites that have provided information. Even the simplest sites deserve this treatment. Think of the World Wide Web as the product of electronic publishing.

Every Web site is essentially produced by a "publisher," be it an individual in Ecuador, a nonprofit organization in Egypt, a multinational corporation in Malaysia, or a state university in the United States. Each of these publishers deserves the same respect and courtesy that one would offer a print publisher. Translated: Writers can "borrow" some materials, but they had better not steal.

How

As already indicated, to provide the "how-to" for every variety of Web document would require a separate handbook. The best advice is to consult a resource such as the *MLA Handbook for Writers of Research Papers* (Gibaldi, 1999), which was updated in 1999 to include every electronic resource one could imagine as of that date. For now, what's most important is to emphasize approaching all Web documents as if they are texts of some kind. Although it may initially seem strange, think of a clip from a song or movie, a photograph from an online exhibit, a cartoon from an online magazine, as well as personal and professional essays as texts. As such, they deserve fair treatment; writers who borrow them are responsible for giving credit where credit is due. Perhaps the most effective way to teach this is by asking students to make a list of Web documents and see which of them they think need to be cited. Although they may quickly list online books, articles, and essays, they may not think of the previous items. They might also overlook the need for citing databases or "collections" that don't seem to have an author. This should prompt an important discussion about intellectual property and online resources.

Rather than focus on individual Web documents, it is helpful to consider larger sources of information on the Web. The MLA guidelines for citing information databases and scholarly projects offer the following checklist:

Title of the project or database (italicized)

Name of the editor of the project or database (if given)

Electronic publication information, including version number (if relevant and if not part of the title), date of electronic publication or of the latest update, and name of any sponsoring institution or organization

Date of access and network address (Gibaldi, 1999, p. 180)

It's worth noting that the MLA guidelines end with this clever bit of counsel: "If you cannot find some of this information, cite what is available" (Gibaldi, 1999). In other words, a student who discovers information published on March 10, 2006, from the Cable News Network's collection, "CNN Interactive," may not find an author or page numbers. However, if that student downloads the information on July 9, 2006, he or she can, at the very least, help readers locate the source with a notation like this:

CNN Interactive. 10 March 2006. Cable News Network. 9 July 2006. (http://www.cnn.com).

■ CIVIL LITERACY CHALLENGE 1

Borrowing Without Stealing

1. Give students the information in Figure 2.2 about physical and intellectual property.

Figure 2.2

Physical and Intellectual Property

Physical Property. Imagine spending several hours each day, over the course of several weeks, creating something unique. Perhaps it is a small, wooden cabinet with specially designed shelves and drawers. You design it to suit a particular space in your house and fulfill a specific purpose. You do the best you can to make it both functional and handsome, trying out different finishes before you get it to match the room it will occupy in your house. It may not be the finest piece of carpentry you have ever seen, but it is yours, and you are justifiably proud of it. How would you feel if someone came along and "borrowed" it without asking your permission?

Intellectual Property. Now imagine spending just as many hours, over the course of several weeks, creating a Web site. It's your first Web site, with links to original pictures you've drawn and essays that you've written. You've spent countless hours refining those essays, scanning the pictures, and creating a "look" that is both visually appealing and helpful. You admit it's not the finest Web site on the Internet, but it is yours, and you are proud of it. How would you feel if someone came along and "borrowed" those pictures and essays without asking your permission?

"Borrowing" intellectual property without the creator's permission is a serious matter. In fact, it is *theft*. What's more, it's a violation of your school's policies on academic honesty, and it could lead to serious problems. Perhaps you've discussed the issue of plagiarism (presenting other people's words or ideas as if they're your own) with respect to print materials. If so, you have learned to document sources of information, giving credit where credit is due. It should come as no surprise, then, that you must do the same thing for sources of information on the Web.

For example, while no one owns the "idea" of a Web site, individual creators own the rights to their creation. *The Cyberpilot's License* Web site, for instance, is a unique expression of relatively common ideas and principles. Although linking to this site is not a violation of intellectual property rights, "borrowing" the original exercises you find there without giving proper credit would most certainly be a violation. Make sense? If not, take a moment to discuss the ideas of plagiarism and academic honesty with your teacher, then proceed to the next section.

2. Present this scenario to students:

When in doubt, document that source! Let's say you are writing a short research paper for class. You go to the library and discover some useful information in an encyclopedia. It's perfect for your essay, but you want to provide proper references. No problem. You know how to cite information from an encyclopedia, right? Good. However, what if that's the only information you can find on your topic in a printed source? What if the rest of your sources are all electronic ones? What if you want to use one or more of the following, which are among the most common sources of information available to online researchers?

- Private e-mail
- Mailing list messages
- Newsgroup messages
- Synchronous communication (MUDS, MOOs, IRCs)
- World Wide Web message boards
- Web sites and databases

3. Give students a few minutes to think about the following questions. Then ask them to write a response to each for the electronic sources listed, and prepare to discuss their responses with classmates.
   a. What special considerations should you give to these electronic sources? In other words, what is unique about these sources? What defines them?
   b. Why must you provide documentation for these sources?
   c. How should one cite each of these sources?

4. In small groups or as a full class, ask students to discuss what they have written and make a list of other electronic resources that require proper documentation when used as secondary sources. Finally, encourage students to identify parallels between print and electronic sources while investigating different approaches to the citation of online sources. To arrange the latter, have them consult different style manuals and handbooks, including online reference material like the Internet Public Library's archives for citing electronic resources (http://www.ipl.org/div/farq/netciteFARQ .html). Discuss the variations in these guidelines, noting the patterns that emerge as well as the differences that exist. As is often the case, establishing the conceptual framework—a rationale for documentation of electronic sources—encourages students to obey what often feels like an unwritten rule, but remains a fundamental requirement for scholarly communities.

Teacher's Tip

Although limited in scope, this exercise helps students understand the significance of respecting intellectual property. The items selected for discussion are some of the most frequently used without proper documentation. Because some sources are less formal and are not considered "published," students may overlook the need for citations. However, if teachers return to the rhetorical heart of computer literacy and reiterate the need for civil literacy, students will learn that borrowing ideas from informal and unpublished sources can damage one's ethos just as much as borrowing from formal, published sources. Although students should have fewer problems understanding the need for documentation of online books, magazine articles, and essays, it is the "gray area" of these interpersonal messages that teachers need to address to strengthen students' civil literacy skills.

■ CIVIL LITERACY CHALLENGE 2

Putting out the Flames

Although intellectual property rights remain controversial and ambiguous, the second major concern of civil literacy depends largely on common sense and respect for individuals rather than for their property. As everyone knows, in real life, there are many ways to offend, humiliate, and hurt others. The same is true online. However, what's different in this environment is that participants cannot see the physical reaction of their audience. Without the visual cues that people have learned to "read" on human faces—the blushing of embarrassed cheeks, the furrowing of an angry brow, the widening of offended eyes—how can young writers determine whether their words have given offense? If offended, what should an individual do? How do participants communicate wounded feelings without escalating tensions? Perhaps a civil literacy challenge dedicated to online "flame wars" will help.

What to Do

1. Present this scenario to students:

    Imagine this: After many hours of researching, composing, and revising, you have filed your first online report for a school tele-computing project that asks you and your classmates to correspond with students around the world. You have put a lot of yourself into this work, and you are proud of what you've accomplished. You are eager to hear what other participants think of the report, although you're a little nervous as well. So the arrival of an e-mail response the very next day leaves you breathless. The message reads as follows:

    > I just read the report you submitted to the discussion forum. I thought the first paragraph was kind of informative, but the rest of the report is dull and useless. You base most of what you write on observations and personal experience, which makes it pretty egotistical and boring. To tell you the truth, I didn't see the point. If this weren't a school project, I would've quit reading after the first paragraph. I think you should back up your opinions with facts; it would make your report more believable and interesting. I don't have any questions because there wasn't anything there that I didn't already know.

2. Ask students how they would reply to this message. Perhaps the best way to answer that question is to have students ask another one: What sort of dialogue would they like to have with this individual? A message of this sort often leads to what's called a "flame war" in cyberspace, the equivalent of a "put-down" session on the playground. The "cyberbullies" who thrive on this activity are cousins to playground bullies and often are just as cowardly, insensitive, and irresponsible. So how does one defuse the situation?

What strategies might put out the flames in cyberspace before the possibility of meaningful discussion is destroyed?

3. To help students consider a range of possibilities, have them consider four fairly common reactions to a message of this sort. They are not the only possible reactions, just four of the most common. Ask students to have a sheet of paper and pen or pencil at hand, so they may respond to each of the options as they are presented. Give students each option in turn.

   a. Option 1: Fight Fire With Fire. In this option, the recipient of the original message adopts a confrontational approach:

> What gives you the right to speak to me like that? To tell *you* the truth, "egotistical" doesn't begin to describe your response to my report. OK, so maybe it didn't have enough facts to please you, but I put a lot of time and effort into that report, and I don't think anyone has the right to call it "dull and useless" or even "boring." I can't wait to see your report. It's probably full of "dull and useless" facts that really bore the life out of a reader. You just wait, Mr. Egotistical. You'll get yours!

Student Preparation

Have students write, on a separate sheet of paper, what they think would happen if they sent a reply like this. Will their correspondent meet "fire with fire" or take a different approach? What will they, in turn, do after they have heard the response?

Responses to Fire

When students have finished, ask them to share their "Responses to Fire" reactions. Unfortunately, hostile replies are an all-too-common response to inflammatory messages. It's unfortunate, because they seldom resolve conflicts. Nonetheless, we're all human, and sometimes emotions get the better of us. So, let's consider three potential reactions to a message like this and prepare to discuss them with students.

Flame on! There's a good chance your "Fire" reply will invite a similar one, which means you're about to get caught in a nasty verbal exchange commonly known as a flame war. Is this what you really want? Is it worth expending time and energy on potentially destructive ends? Be prepared for those flames to climb even higher, and decide whether you intend to toss gasoline or water onto them in the next round.

Apology or Clarification. If you receive an apologetic message, clarifying the previous remarks, then it's your turn to eat humble pie and apologize for your fiery response! Who knows, that first message may have been written by a bored, distracted, or lazy writer who forgot that a real person would take offense to it. Now then, shouldn't you douse the flames and start anew?

Silence. Hmmm . . . always a hard one to read, particularly when you don't know your correspondent. Perhaps he or she is ignoring you? Perhaps he or she didn't even see the message? Or perhaps this indicates thoughtful reflection, which is seldom a bad thing. Regardless, if the silence continues, and you feel somewhat guilty for your strong response, then you may wish to send a follow-up message in a few days' time. If this, too, meets with silence, it's probably best to move on and let bygones be bygones.

b. Option 2: Dousing the Flames. In this option, perhaps you would rather not fight fire with fire. After all, your correspondent may not realize the tone of that first message was offensive. What if this person isn't a good writer or lacks the vocabulary and skills necessary to communicate in a tactful, sensitive manner? If so, this could be your chance to educate that individual, express a candid reaction to the offensive message, and initiate a more thoughtful dialogue. So, imagine that you try to douse the flames by sending a response like the following:

> I was upset by your response to my report. Perhaps I took it too personally, but I think you overstated things a bit, and it hurts to have someone call my work "dull and useless." I admit it wasn't the best report in the world, but it was the best I could do the first time around. I'd appreciate it if in the future you'd refer more specifically to the report. Which facts did you find "informative" and useful? Where did you find it "egotistical and boring?" We're all trying to learn from our mistakes, aren't we? So I'd appreciate it if in the future you could "show, not tell" what you mean—as well as use a kinder, gentler tone.

Student Preparation

Have students write, on a separate sheet of paper, what they think will happen if they send this reply. Will their correspondent respect their attempt to douse the flames like this? What will they do after they have heard a response?

Responses to Dousing the Flames

When students have finished, ask them to share their hypothetical reactions. This type of response to an inflammatory message is more effective if the goal is communication rather than revenge. Once again, there are three fairly common responses to a message like this; students should be prepared for each of them.

Flame on! If a response this genuine and heartfelt meets with another offensive statement, you're obviously dealing with someone who wants to incite a flame war. You should consult with your teacher about this matter and refrain from further attempts to communicate with the individual until there's a significant change in tone and treatment. Until you have established mutual respect, there can be no genuine communication with this individual, and until there's genuine communication, there will be no educational discourse. So why bother? Devote your energies to more productive discussions. Don't let yourself be dragged into a nasty flame war.

Apology or Clarification. More than likely, your response will invite some form of apology or clarification. Perhaps your correspondent was just going through the motions of a homework assignment, typing a flippant reply without thinking of its impact on you. Perhaps he or she didn't give much thought to the tone of the words or your interpretation of them. If that's the case, and the reply to your message at least tries to clarify the cause of the original one (if not apologize for it), then it's wise to move on. You can establish a healthier discourse by acknowledging the clarification, saying that you're grateful for the writer's consideration, and then demonstrating the kind of discussion you'd like to have.

Silence. This is often an indication that the other party needs time to think about things. Let him or her. If a reply comes, it will probably be one of the previous types. If there's no reply, however, you may wish to send a one-liner after a few days. Your correspondent may choose to ignore that as well, but at least you will have defended yourself and your position without adding to the flames. If the silence becomes permanent, you're probably right to read this as confusion on the part of your correspondent. Perhaps he or she is not accustomed to being confronted in this manner. Perhaps he or she is too proud to admit they were wrong and apologize. Or perhaps your tone was so disarming that it left the writer confused. It's best not to rub anyone's face in his or her past mistakes, but if and when this individual surfaces, take note of his or her tone. If it's still nasty, then he or she probably has not learned from this encounter and will need another dose of civil literacy. However, if he or she is deferential, offering thoughts in a more polite and respectful manner, take that as a sign that your effort to douse the flames not only succeeded, but helped alter the discourse as well.

  c. Option 3: The Silent Treatment. Actions, they say, speak louder than words. Yet what is an "action" in cyberspace? What constitutes an "action" in an online discussion? In a virtual community of inquiry, in which one can only act through written statements, there are only two ways to make a statement. These statements are the actions that will define a writer in the community of inquiry. What are they? The obvious action is a written message, but there is another way to make a statement—one that is subtler but may prove very effective in putting out the flames. The "silent treatment" requires that a writer do nothing more than listen and refrain from the active responses described by the first two options (fighting and dousing). So, imagine the response to the original, offensive message looks like this:

- - - - - - - - - - - - -

Student Preparation

  Have students, on a separate sheet of paper, write down what they think will happen if they simply ignore the original message. Will their correspondent meet silence with silence or send another message? What strategies might students adopt if another fiery message comes their way? What if an apology follows? What if nothing comes their way?

Responses to Silence

When students have finished, ask them to share their hypothetical reactions to "Responses to Silence." Yes, silence is a response. It is often an eloquent one, too, full of meaning. Sometimes the most effective way to deal with cyberbullies is to simply ignore them. Easier said than done? Perhaps, but when one is pondering what to do about a nasty message, don't forget that silence is an action in cyberspace, and sometimes the most appropriate one. Once more, consider three common responses to a statement of silence, and discuss them with students.

Flame on! In rare cases, involving the most jaded or immature cyberpunks, your silence could incite another hostile remark ("What's the matter? Did I hurt your feelings or something?"). You could choose to ignore that as well, or else state your position as firmly and carefully as possible, indicating that you do not wish to engage in this kind of discourse. Ultimately, if you want to build a dialogue, you have to devise strategies for dealing with people who are brusque, insensitive, or offensive. Fighting fire with fire may provide immediate gratification, but it may ultimately come back to haunt you. Tread carefully.

Apology or Clarification. If your silence invites an apology or clarification, you are most likely dealing with someone who didn't mean offense in that first message, but who now senses that you took it. So, if the silent treatment is met with a brief message, perhaps a "hello" or "hope you didn't take that the wrong way...," then it makes sense for you to reply, stating the reason for your silence and establishing the kind of dialogue you wish to participate in.

Silence. If silence begets silence, you must now determine what it is that you want. How is one to interpret a silent response to one's own silence? As this is your first interaction with this correspondent, perhaps you were premature in judging those remarks? What if no malice was intended? Perhaps now that you've allowed your emotions to calm themselves, you can send a brief message, stating your initial reaction and establishing a kinder, gentler dialogue. Then again, if you found the original message truly offensive or obscene, perhaps it's best to just let the flames die without stirring the embers.

> d. Option 4: Full-Group Discussion. Clearly, this scenario describes more than an isolated incident between two people. Indeed, episodes like these involve an entire community. The moment a personal message enters a public discussion forum, it becomes everyone's concern. Depending on the situation, students may wish to discuss this matter with their classmates before taking action online. Rather than taking it personally, present it to the class as a community issue. What sort of action would students recommend? What kind of discourse do they wish to encourage? What should others do if an unwanted flame war arises and, in spite of their efforts to douse or ignore the inflammatory messages, it persists?

Ultimately, one of the challenges of communicating through electronic words is learning how to read messages from virtual strangers, interpreting the meaning of the message as well as the intent of the messenger. Without the aid of facial expressions, body language, or tone of voice, it is sometimes difficult to determine a writer's intention. Did the author mean to be rude, or was he or she simply insensitive to the audience? As a general rule, it is best to give people the benefit of the doubt, but if students encounter someone who wants to engage in a flame war, it's best to consider where that might lead. If attempts to douse the flames don't succeed, the silent treatment might be the best course of action. Consider a variation on the golden rule as it is applied to cyberspace interactions: "Write unto others as you would have them write unto you." Unfortunately, not everyone shares this belief—and even those who do often forget to live by it. Students need to devise strategies for dealing with people who wish to incite a flame war and provoke a strong reaction. Rather than fleeing from such problems, advise students to approach them as opportunities to discuss the rules and regulations an online community should establish. How, for instance, does a group maintain civil literacy while discussing controversial issues? Chapter 5 returns to such questions when it broaches the concerns of community literacy.

3

Discourse Literacy

Beyond the Chat Room

By the time students enter a networked computer classroom, many have already experienced online chat rooms, newsgroups, and discussion forums on their own. For the classroom teacher, this can be both a blessing and a curse. The blessing? Such students may understand the technical concerns, bringing a comfort level and familiarity to class sessions that makes it easier for teachers to introduce new learning activities. The curse? This could also mean that students have acquired some unfortunate discursive habits. In other words, teachers have their work cut out for them if they wish to encourage inquiry and dialogue, the prerequisites to a healthy learning environment. What has to happen, ultimately, is that the teacher must address the importance of discourse literacy, reminding students that often what matters most is "not what you say, but how you say it." Just as teachers remind students that the language of the playground is inappropriate in a classroom, students must now distinguish between the discourse of informal chat rooms and that of online discussions in class.

In some cases, using inappropriate discourse is harmless and unintentional, the kind of problem that teachers of adolescents come to expect. Just as they sometimes drag playground discourse into the classroom, students are likely to carry chat room discourse into educational online discussions. This reveals an important distinction, however. When teachers conceive of online learning activities—whether conducted via e-mail, discussion forums, newsgroups, or some other medium—they tend to think of them as writing activities. Thus, the rules of grammar, along with the decorum one expects of written correspondence, apply. However, adolescents who have spent time in chat rooms or in a multiuser domain have a very different orientation. They often think of these activities as conversations, attaching to them the less rigid rules of spoken language. Thus, a potential conflict exists between the expectations that students and teachers bring to these activities, particularly when there is confusion over the type of discourse in which they are engaged. This is especially true when teachers arrange informal brainstorming activities that use online tools for synchronous rather than asynchronous discussions.

These types of discussions are fairly common now, but that does not mean that the tools or the rules for playing with them have been mastered. Synchronous conversations are those that take place in real time. That is, participants are able to contribute at the same moment in time, allowing for interruptions and dialogical discourse. Examples of synchronous conversations are face-to-face discussions in a conventional classroom, telephone calls, Internet Relay Chats, and a variety of synchronized discussions arranged through a networked computer lab. These activities encourage a less-formal discourse, drawing as they do on cultural expectations of spoken language. However, asynchronous conversations present different connotations and expectations. One tends to think of these as descendants of written language, obeying the rules and regulations of a more deliberate and formal discourse. Electronic mail, discussion forums, newsgroups, and electronic bulletin boards fall into this category, because they allow the writer/speaker to compose statements in the absence of an audience. The turn taking here does not allow for interruptions, which means each participant has an opportunity to speak without pause, inspiring declamations as well as dialogues.

Perhaps the greatest challenge for classroom teachers, however, is deciding what to do when students confuse these two discursive styles. Students may think they have expressed themselves in an appropriate manner, only to discover that others find the form and substance of their remarks offensive and inappropriate. If this is especially true of synchronous online discussions, does it mean that classroom teachers should simply avoid them? Is it possible to use such activities for learning purposes? Is it impossible for students to break the bad habits acquired while speaking under the cover of anonymity in chat rooms that may breed irresponsible behavior and discourse?

These are difficult questions, but perhaps the answer to them lies within the study of a literacy that goes to the rhetorical heart of this book. A fundamental prerequisite for reading and interpreting online discourse as well as composing and presenting ourselves in a manner consistent with our intention is discourse literacy (see Figure 3.1). By no means confined to online activities, it is nonetheless essential for communication and learning in these environments.

Figure 3.1

Discourse Literacy

Discourse literacy is the ability to read, understand, and abide by norms that govern the discursive practices of a particular social group.

Before answering some of the questions concerning synchronous online discussions, let us first address rhetorical concerns that challenge students in any writing environment. One of the most difficult concepts for young writers to comprehend is the idea of "voice." They often reveal both ignorance and naïveté when encouraged to use a more natural voice in their writing. "How can I have a voice when I write?" they ask. And yet, all writers most certainly have a voice. But how can teachers "show" what they would otherwise "tell" ineffectively? How can they "hold a mirror up to nature," as it were, and help students see themselves in their own prose?

DISCOURSE LITERACY CHALLENGE 1 ■

Hearing Voices

One way to introduce voice is to examine various authors' writing styles, taking note of the diction, sentence structure, and qualities that identify them.

What to Do

1. For this exercise, teachers should select four different authors with distinctive writing styles.

2. Divide the class into eight small groups (three to four students per group). Each group draws the name of an author from a hat; two groups focus on each of the respective authors.

3. Ask each group to type a representative paragraph from their author (250 words or less).

4. After they have saved the original file on diskette, each group italicizes modifiers, underlines figures of speech, and counts the average number of words per sentence. They save this file as the "original."

5. Then, each group rewrites the paragraph by replacing each of the modifiers with a synonym, selecting different figures of speech, and altering sentence lengths to see how this affects the writing style and voice of the piece.

6. When the groups have finished, ask them to give an oral presentation of the original paragraph, followed by an analysis of it and an oral presentation of the revised passage.

When students begin to "hear voices" in writing, they are ready to experiment with different writing styles and refine their discursive practices. The ability to distinguish various writing styles enables students to discover their own personal voice, which will serve them well in online discussions. Until they do so, however, their protests of poor grades recite a familiar

Teacher's Tip

Ask students if they can see how one creates a voice as a writer and why each word and phrase must be carefully considered because of its contribution to the writer's style and the impact of that voice on an audience. In other words, bring them back to the rhetorical heart of this matter. What the students did, essentially, was to alter the pathos of their paragraph, beginning with all the words and phrases that produce an emotional reaction. This would affect the writer's ethos in some way, because credibility is earned one word at a time, and it would perhaps even alter the logos of the message. The point? Words and expressions define the writer. As the discussion of civil literacy revealed, words are actions in cyberspace. Writers are responsible for those actions and their impact on others. So before jumping into chat rooms and discussion forums, it is a good idea to gain greater control of one's writing voice. Unless students understand that they have a voice as a writer and that it can affect others deeply, they will lack the discourse literacy necessary to temper that voice.

chorus: "I know the writing style's weak, but what about the content?" What they fail to understand, due to limited discourse literacy, is that style and content cannot be separated.

■ DISCOURSE LITERACY CHALLENGE 2

Imitating Voices

The following literacy challenge helps students see how style shapes content, altering the reader's experience of a story.

What to Do

1. To begin, ask students to imagine an incident that involves three or four people. It should be a minor incident, one that can be told in 250 words or less. This will help them focus on writing style more than on plot or character development. Give the students part of one class period to write the story.

2. If possible, locate a copy of Raymond Queneau's (1981) *Exercises in Style* to see how his playful approach to style shapes his story and to pick up ideas on different stylistic approaches that students might adopt. In his book, Queneau provides 99 variations on a simple theme:

   The narrator is on the S bus at rush hour.

   He notices a young man with a long neck wearing a hat.

   The young man is annoyed with someone beside him and says he's bumping into him.

   Finally, the young man sees a vacant seat and takes it.

   Two hours later, the narrator sees the same man at the Gare Saint Lazare. He's with a friend who says, "You ought to get an extra button put on your overcoat." The friend shows him where and explains why. (Queneau, 1981)

3. Share a few of Queneau's (1981) styles with students, then instruct them to write a second version of their story, this time using an entirely different voice. If they are at a loss, encourage them to tell the story from a different point of view or a different frame of mind. What if the narrator were agitated? Amused? Bewildered? Horrified? What if the story were told by someone other than the narrator? In Queneau's story, one could have fun telling the incident from the perspective of the bus driver or the young man wearing the hat.

4. After this retelling, students play "musical chairs" and shift to adjacent computer terminals at short intervals to analyze their classmates' stories, applying some of the techniques acquired from Discourse Literacy Challenge 1 to examine the voice of the original as well as the revised version.

Expanding the Challenge

Ask the students to return to their own narrative and write yet another version, employing yet another voice. Depending on the age group, one could ask that they adopt a particularly bad writing style—passive voice, redundant and verbose language, sentence fragments, and so forth—to help the students see how such poor practices interfere with communication. In a networked classroom, one could also ask students to continue a classmate's narrative, similar to Media Literacy Challenge 3 in Chapter 1. By purposely adopting different styles, and by increasing their sensitivity to language and voice, students will begin to develop the discourse literacy necessary for successful interactions in online writing environments.

Teacher's Tip

This exercise can be conducted in a computer lab without network capabilities. In such instances, students can play musical chairs by shifting to the terminal on their left (or right) to read what a classmate has written. If network capabilities exist, students can post their writing to a class folder or bulletin board, where others may read and respond to the pieces.

GREATER EXPECTATIONS: ■
SYNCHRONOUS ONLINE DISCUSSIONS

The previous exercises could be conducted in a conventional classroom, but a networked computer class enables activities that are cumbersome in a traditional setting. If teachers manage this learning environment properly, and students bring a collaborative spirit to the activities, the class will enjoy writing workshop exercises that were often difficult with slate chalkboards and overhead projectors. To illustrate this point, consider student interaction in a new medium—synchronous online discussions. To succeed in this environment, students must understand that their voice affects the tone of the discourse. For discourse to remain civil, even amid discussion of controversial subjects, they must be sensitive to word choice, writing style, and the tone of voice engaged in the conversation.

At this point, the reader might wish to raise a few important questions. Why bother? What can be accomplished with synchronous online discussions? Are they really worth the trouble? In response, one could argue that this type of activity improves the chances for student participation in class discussions while decentralizing the discourse. In other words, the teacher and impulsive speakers no longer dominate the discussion. This can be exciting and intimidating for teachers as well as students, so comfort levels should dictate one's approach to the activity. If done well, synchronous discussions facilitate small-group discussions and help students refine their reading, writing, and discourse literacy skills. Nonetheless, do not overlook the challenges, which begin with technical concerns but quickly turn into questions about healthy discursive practices and pedagogical strategies. What is acceptable in this environment? If students begin to disparage one another or engage in the rough-and-tumble rhetoric of online chat rooms, what can teachers do besides pull the plug on the exercise?

As with many classroom activities, the teacher sets the tone and models the desired behavior. Before introducing students to synchronous discussions for brainstorming or exploring ideas, it is important that teachers establish greater expectations than students bring to informal chat rooms.

With this in mind, it is a good idea to write a prompt in advance, something that will focus the discussion. If the teacher says, "Okay, let's log on and talk about last night's reading," students may think anything goes. Unless tightly focused, the exercise may deteriorate into a social gathering where flippancy and digression become the norm.

Consider the following example, taken from the start of an actual synchronous exchange in a classroom. In this instance, students were asked to discuss whether they thought of writing as a private or a social act. What the reader sees is precisely what the participants in this online discussion saw scrolling up their computer screens at the start of this synchronous session. Because they were simultaneously composing, reading, and submitting messages, the conversation forfeited the linear qualities of a reciprocal, face-to-face discussion, as indicated by delayed responses to certain threads of the conversation. Notice that a casual approach to grammatical concerns—punctuation, spelling, capitalization, and so forth—accompanies a casual approach to the discourse and exercise.

Howage S.:	hey
Paul M.:	hello all
Lauren G.:	writing is communication, and communication is social
Howage S.:	thats deep
Paul M.:	who thought denver would win?????
Liz E.:	how can thinking be considered social? talking is social, but thinking is personal
Hee L.:	how was the super bowl?
Samuel F.:	It is my belief that writing and especially thinking are personal acts.
Howage S:	it did not surprise me
Liam F.:	i think one way writing is a social act is that we share ideas in either a classroom or with our friends
Wayne:	ok. . . . I didn't read the assignment, so can yall fill me in?

Notice the mixture of discourse styles and subject matter. In many ways, this discussion sets an unfortunate precedent, one that this particular session may not overcome. The teacher not only has forfeited control of the conversation, but also may have invited discourse habits that mirror online chat rooms more than thoughtful classrooms. An intelligent prompt with guiding questions would have helped to establish a sense of purpose and to illustrate the kind of inquiry and discourse the teacher wished to inspire. Although it cannot ensure that students will stay on task, a good prompt can at least give them a sense of direction, a purpose that helps define expectations and boundaries. The inaugural session should place the concern of discourse literacy and the creation of a community of writers at the foreground. Thus, the following prompt for a synchronous discussion using "Interchange," a feature of the Daedalus Integrated Writing Environment, encouraged students to reflect on their reading and share their reactions to it by addressing open-ended questions:

> I'd like to use this first Interchange session to discuss some ideas that your readings have introduced. In "The Writing Community" Ramage and Bean made the following claim: "Behind the notion of the writing community lies the notion that thinking and writing are social acts" (1998, p. 435). Did this claim surprise you in any way? Have your own experiences encouraged you to conceive of thinking and writing as "social acts" or private, personal acts?

If the inaugural session establishes good discourse practices, it will be much easier for future sessions to stimulate healthy discussions, allowing students to "think out loud" and explore ideas in a more open-ended manner. The following prompt is a good example of how one can use synchronous conversations to continue previous discussions, especially ones that failed to open the inquiry and inspire students to question their assumptions. In this instance, the teacher wanted students to reconsider some of the positions they had previously taken. The teacher hoped that by doing this in an online, synchronized forum, students would explore their positions more openly than they had during face-to-face discussions:

> In class on Monday, one of you claimed that a definitional argument could become a "boring" discussion of "semantics." I'm not sure what was meant by "boring" or "semantics," nor am I sure the speaker had clear definitions in mind, so I thought we'd use this session to brainstorm a little, helping one another consider terms worth investigating. You're free to pursue this in whatever manner you wish, but it might help to begin by offering a term that you think needs to be defined more clearly. Why is it important to define that term? It may help to reflect on the following passage from your text before you begin: "For some people, all this concern about definition may seem misplaced. How often, after all, have you heard people accuse each other of getting bogged down in "mere semantics?" But how we define a given word can have significant implications for people who must either use the word or have the word used on them." (Ramage & Bean, 1998, p. 204)

After an inaugural session, it is often wise to print out the transcript and ask students to "perform" the text as if it were a script. This reinforces the importance of civil literacy, holding everyone accountable for his or her words. Although the decentralized discourse of a synchronous discussion is liberating and often enables shy students to speak more than they would in conventional class discussions, teachers should not allow students to indulge in discursive habits that would not be tolerated in face-to-face sessions. The following prompt was offered at the start of a synchronous discussion immediately after the previous one. In this instance, the teacher merges both the medium for this conversation and its topic, asking students to question the medium while using it to facilitate their conversation:

> I thought we'd conduct our "definitional argument" on Interchange today. This seems appropriate, since we'll argue the following: "Interchange is/is not communication." Now that you've had a chance to review your group's previous Interchange session, discuss the meaning of "communication" in our discussion forum, and reflect on various issues, what's your opinion? Does an Interchange session meet your definition of "communication" or not? Please take a position, presenting an "enthymeme" as well as the warrant, backing, and grounds of your argument. You should also be prepared to discuss the conditions of rebuttal, qualifiers, and questions.

Obviously, curricular obligations do not allow teachers to dedicate all of their time to discussions of instructional technology. In most instances, teachers need to use computers as a vehicle for the study of other topics, not as the subject itself. How might teachers stimulate thoughtful, topical discussions in synchronous online sessions? Often, it is simply a matter of asking questions that encourage students to take their own ideas and questions seriously. The following prompt tries to do just that, asking students to generate their own questions to form an online community of inquiry as they respond to a difficult reading assignment. Notice the way in which the teacher uses an excerpt from the reading to focus the students' attention, followed by questions that are meant to stimulate open-ended inquiry:

> Your passage from Plato's (2000) *Republic* comes at the conclusion of his famous "allegory of the cave." To refresh your memories, both now and in the future, here is the passage:
>
> "This entire allegory, I said, you may now append, dear Glaucon, to the previous argument; the prison house is the world of sight, the light of the fire is the sun, and you will not misapprehend me if you interpret the journey upward to be the ascent of the soul into the intellectual world according to my poor belief, which, at your desire, I have expressed—whether rightly or wrongly, God knows. But, whether true or false, my opinion is that in the world of knowledge the idea of good appears last of all, and is seen only with an effort; and, when seen, is also inferred to be the universal author of all things beautiful and right, parent of light and of the lord of light in this visible world, and the immediate source of reason and truth in the intellectual; and that this is the power upon which he who would act rationally either in public or private life must have his eye fixed." (Plato)
>
> Now then, let's begin with your questions. What questions do you have about this passage? What don't you understand, but would like to clarify in your own mind? What would you like to discuss?

Although this approach works well with students who enjoy asking their own questions, there are occasions when the teacher may wish to be more directive, particularly with a group that loses focus or interprets the intellectual freedom of open-ended questions as an invitation to turn a serious discussion into an undisciplined chat session. The following prompt, therefore, was designed to focus students' attention on concerns that the teacher wished to discuss about a film adaptation. In this instance, the teacher wanted to make certain that students had "read" the film carefully, before shifting to a more open-ended discussion of thematic concerns. By setting a time limit, meanwhile, the teacher hoped to focus the discussion on the text, limiting digressions that could subvert the exercise:

> Ray Bradbury's novel, *Fahrenheit 451*, depicts a utopian society that some might consider dystopian. Before making such judgments, however, it's important to establish the "facts" upon which an argument is founded and explore their causes. As a group, therefore, I'd like you to discuss the following with respect to the film adaptation of this novel. You may address these questions chronologically or simultaneously, but we'll limit this Interchange session to 15 minutes.
>
> What were the most striking rules and customs in this utopian society?
> What caused this society to create such rules and customs?
> What parallels, if any, would you draw between this society and yours?
> What is the implicit "recommendation argument" of this film?

Although important, setting a good example and establishing high standards for online discourse may not be enough. Prompts like these give direction to students, but things can quickly run amok if the teacher fails to moderate the discourse that evolves in either synchronous or asynchronous online forums. This raises a serious concern—one that requires vigilance and, occasionally, intervention on the part of the teacher.

CASE STUDY: PAUL M. ■

What does a teacher do when a student resists instruction, ignores prompts, and generally behaves as if a synchronous, classroom discussion is just another anonymous chat room where anarchy is not only tolerated but encouraged? The same thing that teachers have always done in response to inappropriate behavior: Confront it. In some cases, a difficult individual may need help that the teacher cannot give, but before jumping to conclusions, it is a good idea to talk with the student. More often than not, students are not fully aware of the discursive habits they have acquired through recreational chat sessions. They have grown so accustomed to treating people in disrespectful ways that they do not see any problem with bringing that behavior into an online synchronous discussion in the classroom.

Take, for example, the case of Paul M., the student in the earlier Interchange session who thought it appropriate to discuss the outcome of the Super Bowl rather than the designated topic. When questioned about this, Paul M. simply stated, "That's just my style." When asked how he had acquired it, Paul M. informed his teacher that he had spent a lot of time in chat rooms, where it was acceptable to "flame" others and talk about "whatever comes up." Perhaps most telling, however, was an incident that took place just a short time after this Interchange, during an asynchronous conversation in the Web-based discussion forum the teacher created for the class. The following prompt triggered this incident:

> How has your study of rhetoric, both reading and writing arguments, affected the way you "see" the world? Have you detected any change in the way you watch movies, read the newspaper, participate in conversations, etc.? Do you find yourself filtering the world through new terms such as ethos, pathos, and logos? What does this say about the relationship between your learning and your perception of the world around you?

A short time later, Chris O., a student who rarely spoke in class, posted the following response in the discussion forum:

> After reading and learning about rhetoric, I find myself looking for ethos, logos, and pathos when I watch TV or read the paper. I try to understand what the author or the company is trying to do with their ad or article. I guess this means that I am applying what I have learned to everyday life.

The next response to this thread (as it is called in online discussions) came from Paul M., who chose to remark upon his classmate's comments before addressing his instructor's questions. Pay special attention to the voice of this message, the discourse style of its author, and its attitude toward others:

> Puckered up enough Chris? The way i see things has not been changed at all. i have always seen an advertisement and thought, what are the really tring to say. like that folders, good till the last droop sign on the freeway to houston, i mean that could really screw things up for them, or at least that is what i thought at first, then while my friend and i drove there we sat there and tried to figure out who the sign was for for like 30 min.s, and we did and the sign sticks in my head today, so i guess they did a good job, but i wonder who they are advertising to though. i mean it is not someone who is on there way to work that will sit there and try to figure out what they are tring to say, no it is two board teens on there way to houston that does that, so i guess we are there audience!!!!! TADA, i got lots to say!!!!

When asked about this exchange, Paul M. shrugged nonchalantly and said, "It's no big deal, we do that all the time on the AOL chat room." When asked how he thought Chris O. might feel about this, particularly since Chris O. was a reticent member of the class and not familiar with chat rooms, Paul M. shrugged again, and replied, "It's nothing personal, just words." Clearly, Paul M. had gained the technical skills necessary to participate in online discussions. What he lacked, however, was an understanding of civil literacy and a mature appreciation of discourse literacy. He did not understand his teacher's irritation, nor did he see any reason to apologize to his classmate. What he needed, obviously, was to understand that words are actions and that behind those actions are human beings with human emotions. Although Chris O. never complained, the teacher would have been remiss had he not addressed this incident with Paul M. Although this case may be a bit more extreme than most, there is nothing singular about Paul M.'s extensive experience with uncivil discourse and insensitivity to others. Many students lack discourse literacy, which makes it difficult for them to create or sustain civil conversations online. Once again, teachers cannot flee from this reality, nor should they dismiss the activity or suspend students like Paul M. indefinitely. Rather, they need to approach these occurrences as learning opportunities, raising student sensitivity to discursive practices and their impact on a community of inquiry.

Paul M. never fully reformed, but he did learn to temper his language as the semester progressed. Later Interchange sessions, as well as discussion forum postings, revealed more self-consciousness and respect for his audience. Nonetheless, his earlier contributions had already set an unfortunate precedent, establishing an online persona that would occasionally provoke hostile reactions when Paul M. simply made an appearance in future exchanges. Ironically, Paul M. would point to classmates who indulged in reckless or offensive outbursts against him. Again, the teacher felt obligated to step in at such times and remind students of the "greater expectations" required in order for this activity to serve a useful, educational purpose. However, once the Pandora's box of uncivil discourse has been opened by a member of the online community, it can be difficult to close—particularly when the rest of the group wishes to slam the lid of that box on the culprit's head!

ESTABLISH THE RULES, PLAY BY THE RULES ■

So, what should be done about this? Wringing one's hands or pulling the plug on networked computer technology will accomplish very little. Those are evasive maneuvers, not educational ones. A more appropriate response would establish the rules for discourse locally before turning students loose in telecollaborative projects that involve a wider community. As mentioned previously, printing out a transcript from a synchronous discussion and performing it aloud helps remind students to take responsibility for their words and actions online. From there, the golden rule applies. Whether one is conducting synchronous conversations in a networked classroom or asynchronous conversations on an international level, "Write unto others as you would have them write unto you."

Younger age groups may need more specific guidelines than this, so it is worthwhile to spend a few sessions analyzing discursive practices with them. In general, students are more likely to follow the rules if they understand why they exist, which requires some sense of ownership. Thus, it is mutually beneficial for the teacher to include the students in the rule-making process. One might begin by listing the "turn-ons" and "turn-offs" of online discourse, letting small groups discuss what they find enabling rather than disabling, and defining the steps they might take as a group to limit harmful interactions and hold one another accountable. By starting to establish healthy discursive habits locally, teachers fare better if and when they decide to extend the classroom to a more global conversation. Working through these issues with a group they see in face-to-face sessions helps teachers understand why online discourse sometimes deteriorates into flame wars and monologues rather than developing into civil dialogues.

There are also lessons to be learned about keeping online discussion groups small, writing good prompts for synchronous sessions, and granting students the latitude to play with language and ideas. As always, there is no substitute for experience when it comes to learning these lessons, although pedagogical experiments such as the following may help teachers learn more rapidly.

■ DISCOURSE LITERACY CHALLENGE 3

Role Playing Online

New possibilities introduce new responsibilities and problems. How, for instance, does the teacher prevent students from simply "typing" instead of thinking, reflecting, and writing? If one is not careful, synchronous discussions may become little more than a typing competition, a new discourse in which the privileged ones are the students who type the fastest. As a corrective to this situation, one teacher deliberately slowed the pace of the exchange. Students were given a prompt and asked to compose an opening statement as a separate document, save it on a diskette, and then post it in the forum after a brief period, rather than plunging directly into the fury of a synchronous discussion. At that point, they were required to read all of their classmates' opening statements before typing a response.

What to Do

1. Place in a hat the names of important individuals whom students have encountered during a study unit. These could be political figures from the past or present, famous scientists, mathematicians, artists, or authors.

2. Ask each student to draw one name from the hat and review the readings and class notes about the individual whose name the student drew.

3. Instruct each student to adopt that individual's name and viewpoint for a synchronous or asynchronous discussion. Tell students to keep their "identities" secret.

4. Challenge the students to see how closely they can simulate their character's discourse style and point of view.

■ CASE STUDY: ONLINE ROLE PLAYING

In the following example, students were asked to discuss whether they believed the Internet would lead society to the bliss of cybertopia or the discomforts of cyberbia. Students adopted the identity of authors studied throughout the semester, which compelled closer examination of respective works and their creators. To provide guidelines and inspire thoughtful discussion, the teacher adopted the role of Plato and offered the following prompt.

Plato:	As you know, our group has studied "The Rhetoric of Utopia" for the past three months, investigating the historical roots of utopian rhetoric as well as modern examples of utopian/ dystopian visions. Today, we'd like to hear your views on some controversial issues that speak to the future. You hold a prominent place in current debates over the role of media in society. While many people have noted that ours is an increasingly "mediated" world—that is, a place in which experience and perception are shaped by print and electronic media—there's far less agreement about whether this is good or bad. Where do you stand in terms of this debate, and what would you suggest is necessary to make our "mediated" society more satisfying? We'd also like to know what you think of the prospects for online communities. Imagine, if you will, a society in which all the citizens are online, using e-mail and the Internet on a daily basis. What kind of society do you envision? Is it a brave new world that we might call "cybertopia" or a nightmarish vision called "cyberbia?" What proposal(s) would you offer to help us create the former rather than the latter? Please take a few minutes to compose your thoughts, then post them in your group's Interchange session and wait for your colleagues to post their messages. After you've had a chance to read and reflect upon their visions, please respond to their ideas in dialectical fashion.

Student Dialogue

Students were given approximately 5 minutes to compose their initial thoughts. As a result, their first posting offered a rather static declamation, which would prove critical to subsequent exchanges. By requiring participants to read their colleagues' opening statements before engaging in the synchronous exchange, the teacher hoped to engender a more thoughtful discourse, encouraging critical inquiry and the exploration of ideas. The following excerpt features the opening statements from one discussion group, which involved seven role-playing students. The text appears exactly as the students created it.

Kevin Kelly:	I feel that we should all view the internet as a wonderful phenomenon which brings the world together into one big "family." What would make our "mediated" society more satisfying would be to see everyone participating. We should work as a group in order to progress to the next level of technology. If everyone were online everyday, individuals who thought that they were nothing before could now be someone, helping everyone else in

the community achieve similar goals. I believe that this would be a "cybertopia," but in order for this to occur, people would have to learn to use the internet responsibly.

George Orwell: The image of a society whose perception of reality is the product of a print or electronic-based medium is a frightening one. How is it possible to know who or what is ultimately controlling these information sources? We are told that the organizations which have their names at the top of the page or screen are responsible for all content, but there is no way to be absolutely sure. Human beings need to interact with human beings in order to create a truly meaningful reality. Interaction with information alone and belief or action based on the same makes us slaves to those who disseminate the information. If we do not educate ourselves about the dangers of reliance on media, we are damned. As far as the Internet goes, the result of blind allegiance would be "cyberbia" indeed.

Neil Postman: Our perception is greatly influenced by print and electronic media, but this may be detrimental rather than beneficial. The reason that a "mediated" world may have harmful effects is because we, as consumers and educators of others, have not learned how to use this technology and its implications. We must be careful of the Huxleyan world. People do not take the time out to ask where the information is coming from and what the information is exactly. The best solution I can propose lies within education. We are not going to stop watching television and using the internet so we must learn how to use them. It is the job of the schools to educate our children about this, but that is much harder than it sounds. Schools have never been asked to do this before and the educators themselves may not be prepared to handle such a task.

Sven Birkerts: Considering a large part of our population is run through this vast computer system, I think we are already dealing with the inter net as a daily part of out lives. Our problem lies with the question of why we are using the computer daily. Is it because we are expected to do five tasks at one time? Since time is our problem, we have lost the desire to question where we are and why are we on the computer.

Aldous Huxley: A world in which experience and perception are shaped by print and electronic media will only bring about false happiness and the demise of deeper philosophical thought. As I wrote in my book, Brave New World, the greater the dependence on technological devices to provide pleasure, the shallower people became. In order to preserve this new forum, and prevent it from becoming this "cyberbia," I would propose...an educational program to teach people how to integrate the internet into their lives, and not have it take over their lives.

Howard Rheingold: I am just afraid that the entire world will become so caught up in the fun part of this technology, that they will not question why it has been created. As a questionless society we are succumbing to great pleasure, not realizing that there must be consequences.

By now, six of the seven members of the group had posted their opening statements. The seventh member had been excused for a short period at the start of the session. At this point, the teacher asked the rest of the group to read each other's opening statements and compose replies directed to one of their colleagues. The seventh class member, who was playing the role of Kurt Vonnegut, would post an opening statement and join the discussion in progress after returning.

Kevin Kelly:	Huxley, Don't you think that we can use the internet as a gathering place, to exchange ideas and maybe to implement them? Once we are connected, we are like a bee hive, working together for a common purpose.
George Orwell:	Aldous—I agree with your proposal, but an equally important proposal to go along with teaching people how to integrate the internet into their lives would have to be teaching them what the internet is. Most people are oblivious to the source of information, often with disastrous results.
Howard Rheingold:	Orwell, not to mention that a lot of the information is often bogus and unreliable.
Aldous Huxley:	Kelly, what do you think would happen to individual personas once we all became assimilated into this new "family"? And is achieving that next level of society really going to better society? I believe that grouping these people into a collective will only stifle creative thought. People will not be able to find inspiration in nature, or satisfaction in a one-on-one conversation. And increased technology could lead to the medicalization of society and the development of God complexes amongst the scientists.
Kurt Vonnegut:	Electronic media has the possibility of controlling your mind. Machines and computers do not enhance intelligence. The Internet does not provide a medium which encourages learning, communication or creativity. The Web may approach "cyberbia." Unless we begin to understand what it is and what its purpose is, it will produce the same quality of entertainment as TV. We can ignore it, allowing it to take its course, trusting that future generations will use it more productively than we have. Or we can understand what drives the Internet and TV (corporations, money), and then comprehend what kind of medium this is and what we should use it for. However, it may not be entirely bad. Just as the arrival of paperback books provided a cheap way for unknown authors to be published, so can the Internet provide a place for a community of artists who are able to show their writing, films, paintings and music.
George Orwell:	Kurt—I agree with everything you say. The Internet does have potential, but only if its users know what runs it.
Kurt Vonnegut:	Kelly, you mention that those who have no identity can now have one. However, do you think this is a true identity, or one which they create and wear as a disguise?
Neil Postman:	Orwell, that is precisely what I was talking about. People are blindly following what the internet is offering, without questioning their

sources. Even after obtaining some sort of information, the majority of people using this technology do not know how to use the info they have just gotten.

Kevin Kelly: Aldous, People would still be able to find inspiration in nature, but they will have a new way of sharing it with the rest of the world.

Howard Rheingold: I cannot deny that the internet has brought the entire world one step closer to the brotherhood we are always advocating. There are educational Web sites and places to discuss current laws and proposals on the internet. Vonnegut, I believe that yes we are embracing this much too quickly and with not enough doubt.

Sven Birkerts: Kelly, Think about the term "bee hive." Do we really want to be workers doing our jobs without question. We don't know why we are doing, all we know is it is our place in this technological society.

Plato: Vonnegut, Do you think that all this technology is leading us toward something like the situation you described in your short story, "Harrison Bergeron"?

Kurt Vonnegut: Huxley, I agree that we will become assimilated into this one computer-generated world. We cannot remain individuals while we are personified as names on a screen.

George Orwell: Postman—Not only do they not know how to use it, but they don't know how it (or those that broadcast it) might be using/controlling them.

Kurt Vonnegut: Plato, Yes, I see this technology as having the possibility of controlling our minds instead of us controlling technology. It could give us no identity by making us all equals, equals in that you and I are no different from anyone else.

Neil Postman: Kurt, while the internet can be a place for artists to show their talents, it can also be place where people can publish anything, and therefore deceive the public.

Aldous Huxley: Kelly, why can't we GATHER in person? why must we begin using a false forum? the internet is a false forum b/c we "connect" to other computers, other two-dimensional images and "personas"— not real human beings. All deep meaning can be lost when using a cold, lifeless machine to bring us to other people via an imaginary "highway." Ideas may be exchanged, but we never know where the ideas come from—like they appear from thin air. And once "connected," like a "bee hive," won't we all turn into the working drones, void of individual thought and complying to everything the queen says? Is the bee hive analogy truly a utopian concept? doesn't it just scream hierarchy, loss of individual freedoms?

Howard Rheingold: I agree with all of you. But we must have some faith in the human race. In order to believe in utopias we must believe that there are people who can create them.

Kevin Kelly: Kurt, If people want to make up their own identities, that is possible, but if people are true to themselves and want others to see them as who they are, why would they use disguises?

Sven Birkerts:	We could still question why we would have to do things. The computers would not necessarily be controlling us.
Kurt Vonnegut:	Orwell and Postman: I wonder how we should use the Internet once we understand that it is controlled by money. Do you think it should be entertainment only? The Internet is at essence just a tool; it does what its users tell it to do. What I worry about is the desires of its users—how might THEY want to control our minds.
Neil Postman:	Orwell, true true. That furthers the point that only education can help the situation. Since this technology has already been introduced and so widely accepted, we cannot take it away. Our only choice is to go forth with more knowledge about how to use it wisely.
Kurt Vonnegut:	Birkerts: I hope that people would question why, but I fear that it will become another television, only more frightening, as it has the capability of replacing real life: in virtual reality and video games.
Sven Birkerts:	Do you think the majority of the people using the internet and watching 30–40 hours of television a week step back and ask why they are so addicted to this screen?
Kevin Kelly:	Aldous, Yes, we could GATHER in person, but that group would be so limited. Using the internet, we can expand that group endlessly.
Howard Rheingold:	Nothing can replace real life. There is no exchange for human interaction. However, if introverted, shy people are able to gain confidence because of their voiced opinions on the internet, then they will become more likely to go out in public and share their views.
Kevin Kelly:	Birkerts, I don't think people even realize that they are addicted to the screen.
Kurt Vonnegut:	Kelly: People can use disguises if they are incapable of dealing in social situations. They may see the Internet as a way to "become someone else." Someone who is not incapable of functioning in a social setting. Then, they have ignored the real problem, which is, why can they not act this way in one-to-one conversation?
Sven Birkerts:	Vonnegut: How do you propose we look at and question the mind set of adapting humans?
Aldous Huxley:	Rheingold, should we really have faith? think about the term FAITH: absolute, blind trust; should we have faith in a group of beings that inherently do bad things to one another?
Neil Postman:	Kurt, I think entertainment only would not be beneficial to us. There are great resources provided by the internet. We can find things of value so long as we can determine where the information comes from, that is that it's legitimate.
Howard Rheingold:	Huxley, humans are animals, just as dogs and lions are. Therefore, in order to survive only the fittest go on to live and reproduce. Blind trust is what keeps some people living on a daily basis.
Kurt Vonnegut:	Rheingold: Yes, that's possible, but I also see that these same people could become trapped by the computer, unable to go out

> in their daily lives and reenact the characters they've made on the computer. They become so wrapped up in what's going on with their chat room friends, that they ignore the world outside.
>
> *Plato:*   Postman, good point! How do we make sure that dialectical discourse—something that's on your mind a good deal—is alive and well in cyberspace? How do we prevent it from becoming just another version of television, where people accept information passively instead of interrogating it? Rheingold, would you care to comment as well?

This brief excerpt from one small group's synchronous online discussion reveals a good deal about the potential for this type of learning activity. Clearly, the creation of a thoughtful prompt, allowance for student reflection and composition, and a slow, deliberate start helped generate a rich, intellectual discussion. It should be noted, however, that the teacher did not stumble on such a strategy without a significant number of trials (and even more errors). With experimentation and patience, however, one learns to use synchronous online discussions to stimulate open-ended inquiry and alter the classroom dynamics. Consider, for example, how often every student contributes half a dozen statements during a conventional class discussion. How often do face-to-face discussions enable this kind of decentralized discourse without losing their focus? Of course, the quantity of student participation does not guarantee quality, nor does it mean that every use of synchronous online discussions will be more satisfying than face-to-face ones. Nonetheless, this excerpt demonstrates what can be accomplished when the teacher establishes high expectations and arranges the sessions to help students meet them.

Student Reflections

What do students think of this type of learning activity? Reactions vary, but one of the unanticipated benefits of holding class discussions in a new medium is that it calls attention to the pedagogical strategies that the teacher employs. It is often beneficial for both the students and teacher to write a reflection at the conclusion of such an exercise. In the following examples, students voice both approval and frustration after participating in a synchronous, role-playing discussion online. Consequently, their insights help the teacher consider the influence of online writing activities on individual students and the group as a whole, inspiring reflections on this new learning environment and ideas for future adjustments or innovations.

The Importance of Being Anonymous

> This interchange was very interesting and stimulating. I'm not convinced that the knowledge gained was any better than in previous interchanges, but I know that ours became pretty heated. The frank discussion on the basis of anonymity was amazing, though. However, I'm not sure that everyone in our group was representing

their author's views instead of their personal ones. In our group, the person playing Atwood said that she was a "mentor." This is a small detail to know about a person, and I think I remember someone in our class saying that she was a mentor, so this was a problem. This activity would have been much worse in a face-to-face situation. We know each other now too well to get riled up about these things without anonymity. Also, it was quite difficult to know how authors like ours would respond to the internet; I guess that was part of the brain work involved with this assignment.—Brian E.

The Advantages of Small Groups

Today's interchange session was great. I really enjoyed the role-playing. I think it helped us understand what the authors were trying to say, and it definitely brought up issues that I would have otherwise missed. The past interchange sessions were good, but I liked this one better for several reasons. The other ones seemed too large. I felt like I was saying plenty, but I never felt like I could keep up with the different strands of conversation. This time also, I felt like it made people prepare better. It kind of made us as a group really pay attention to what we were saying since it was as though we were a representation of that person.—Ericka J.

The Significance of Identity

I think that this interchange was very different. Although it allowed people to put up another barrier to their identity, it allowed them to identify themselves through their openness. This environment is good because you have to adopt someone else's view that might not be your own. This helps to make what you believe stronger or change because you consider another viewpoint. I don't think that this would have worked as well in a face-to-face discussion because people would have felt it silly. On the Internet they can hide [their] faces.—Manish C.

Separating Messages From the Messenger

This interchange was different in that it allowed us to understand how others interpret the readings that we have been doing. To argue well one needed to actually think in the way their author would. This required a good grasp of their topic and an understanding of the point the author was trying to make. The interchange was also interesting because it put many famous viewpoints together in a forum that would not be possible otherwise. These authors would never have the chance to argue their point with the others. I think it is better than a face to face interaction because it allows anonymity. We didn't know whom the others were when taking on their persona. This allowed us to better listen to the arguments objectively.—Mike S.

The Constraints of Assumed Identity

> I did not like this interchange. I did not like the idea of speaking someone else's opinions that were not necessarily the same as mine. I think it led to a discussion that was not very real, and I feel like we didn't get much accomplished. This activity, however, would have been less effective in a face to face situation. It is hard to talk and think about something at the same time, which one can do in an interchange.—Nick W.

Suggestions for Improvement

> The interchange worked better this time than in times past. People seemed more prepared to discuss and the role-playing made them think about what they were going to say. The dialogue slowed down a little. On the other hand, the role-playing limited us to a certain extent. We had to conform to the ideas of a person that limited our range of argument. A looser definition of the roles may help. Each person could be a supporter of their author and not necessarily the author himself. In that way the basic idea of the authors could boost our thinking but not limit us to a narrow opinion—which is harder to develop beyond the author's original text. With strict role playing a face-to-face discourse would have ruined the role-playing. I think looser role-playing could be done effectively if in a different manner in each form of discussion.—Kevin W.

■ PERSONAL LITERACY

Discourse literacy—the ability to read, understand, and abide by norms that govern the discursive practices of a particular social group—is obviously a fundamental skill for students in both online and offline discussions. In many ways, it is the beginning of a student's initiation to the world and to the self. Although it is liberating to play roles and emulate another writer's style, point of view, or ideology, at some point, students must come back to themselves. Otherwise, teachers run the risk of pandering to students, providing only the "edutainment" that critics fear. Thus, role playing serves a useful purpose, but its educational value suffers if it becomes an end in itself. At some point, students must graduate from discourse literacy to investigations of themselves and their own views, developing the skills necessary for personal literacy in cyberspace.

4

Personal Literacy

Discovering Oneself Online

Although many students enjoy using pseudonyms in online activities, they should beware of the temptation of incessant role playing, which distances them from their own thoughts, feelings, and identity. The reason for this is that one of the most important questions for adolescents remains a nontechnical one: Who am I? Defining the self, and understanding the forces that shape it, is a lifetime skill that requires personal literacy (see Figure 4.1).

Figure 4.1

> ### Personal Literacy
>
> Personal literacy is the ability to undergo a personal initiation to the self, recognize how others read and perceive that self through social interactions, and understand the social forces that shape an individual's identity.

As with discourse literacy, this did not begin with the advent of cyberspace. Nonetheless, online interactions raise new questions and concerns about individual identity. Students must learn how to create an online persona through the words, expressions, and ideas they put forth; this also requires sensitivity to the way others "read" an individual online, as well as an open-minded exploration of the self. This is no simple feat, of course, particularly for adolescents who are more comfortable playing roles and imitating the discursive styles or viewpoints of others. As Sherry Turkle (1997), a Massachusetts Institute of Technology professor of clinical psychology, observed in *Life on the Screen*, there is a seriousness lurking behind our playful experiments with an online persona, one that students may not fully grasp, but that educators cannot neglect:

> Some are tempted to think of life in cyberspace as insignificant, as escape or meaningless diversion. It is not. Our experiences there are serious play. We belittle them at our risk. We must understand the dynamics of virtual experience both to foresee who might be in danger and to put these experiences to best use. Without a deep understanding of the many selves that we express in the virtual we cannot use our experiences there to enrich the real. If we cultivate our awareness of what stands behind our screen personae, we are more likely to succeed in using virtual experience for personal transformation. (p. 269)

■ INITIATION STORIES

In literature, such transformations are often spoken of as "initiation stories," which focus primarily on two types of situations: initiation to the world and self. Of the two, the latter is far more difficult, particularly for people who are afraid to explore their personal histories, beliefs, and identities. In many ways, this describes adolescents fascinated by images flashing across their computer screens. Educators must help them use the computer to acquire personal literacy, discovering who they are and how others read them online. In the following excerpt from the start of a synchronous online discussion, notice how the teacher's prompt catches several students by surprise. They struggle with the idea of a personal voice, discussed in the previous chapter, as well as the question of self-definition.

Teacher:	In the initial phase of a writing assignment we must discover what we think, working in an "exploratory" fashion. Later, we express those thoughts in "demonstrative" fashion, stating an argument and supporting it. Throughout, the essay itself is a means to an end: greater knowledge and understanding of the world and self. I'd like you to reflect for a moment upon the Definitional Arguments that you just completed. What did you learn about yourself, your topic and other matters during the "exploratory" phase of this project—from topic proposals to group work, research to rough drafts? What did you learn during the "demonstrative" phase while refining your thesis and criteria, locating secondary sources, and revising the final draft of this essay? HOW did you learn these things? Ultimately, how did your work on a definitional argument help define you?
Howard S.:	. . .

Adam J.:	I learned to keep my topic simple
Nick F.:	Before I started my paper I only had a basic knowledge of my topic. After writing and revising the paper I had gone so far as to form a strong opinion about my topic. I also learned a great deal about the nature of education and society
G. J.:	I learned a great deal about my topic. I went into the paper not knowing much about the subject, but finished feeling that I could describe it to someone else.
Adam J.:	if it is not a specific thesis there are too many holes to plug in the essay
Teacher:	Nick, what was your topic?
Howard S.:	I learned that I let the media form my opinion for me on certain issues. I sometimes create my opinion from the biased way they cover a story. After doing the research for my def argument, I was able to find the whole truth instead of the minute bit of truth told by the news the first time I heard about my topic
Jennifer G.:	I learned how to better express my views
Chris O.:	I learned through the topic proposal stage that not all arguments are as easy as they first appear. Defining a language is a lot harder than it seems. I changed my topic to something much simpler, that I already knew about.
Nick F.:	"Meritocracy in Modern America?" was the title to my paper, teach. I discussed the "true" nature of our society and why the US is really not a meritocracy.
Brian K.:	I found that I wasn't really sure how I felt about my issue, capital punishment, and that my opinion changed numerous times. I found that there are a lot of positives as well as a lot of negatives relating to my issue.
Adam J.:	i learned to question the credibility of sources from class . . . it makes all the difference in presenting a persuasive argument
Teacher:	Brian and Howard: I'd be interested to know how you finally found your own "voice" and argument in this essay.
Brian K.:	What exactly is meritocracy?
Chris O:	Howard, yes the left-wing media has a certain way of portraying issues that make it seem simple to understand but when you research the topic you find out that it is different than they portray.
G. J:	Like we said just a minute ago in class, I think everyone goes into a paper with some type of preconceived idea. It's only after you research that you can see that you most likely missed a lot of important ideas concerning the topic.
Nick F.:	Meritocracy is a system by which you are promoted or given credit to based on merit. The military and higher education are examples of this.
Howard S.:	I found my own "voice" from my research
G. J.:	What do you mean by "voice"? I couldn't tell you right now what my voice truly is.

This excerpt from a synchronous, online classroom discussion reveals a good deal about students' perceptions of themselves and the ways those selves are defined. A close reading reveals, among other things, far more comfort talking about the subject of their study and far more knowledge of that subject than of themselves. Although they may volunteer information about their research and interests, most adolescents prove far less generous with insights about their study's impact on themselves. This presents a delicate conundrum for teachers, who must respect a student's right to privacy, which may explain a student's decision not to divulge personal information, while simultaneously encouraging the exploration and reflection that lead to self-knowledge.

■ FOSTERING PERSONAL LITERACY

How do teachers help students acquire personal literacy, developing the ability to read and interpret their words, beliefs, and selves? Although this sort of activity makes some educators uncomfortable, it remains imperative for an online community that wishes to establish civil literacy and hold students responsible for their discursive habits. In effect, teachers must help students examine themselves through critical literacy, an ability to make thoughtful judgments, which derives its meaning from the ancient Greek term *kritikos*. Unfortunately, its modern descendant in mainstream culture, the word *critical*, usually suggests something negative or unflattering. As a corrective, educators must encourage students to think critically, making informed judgments of their own ideas—their origins and expressions—so that they develop personal literacy skills. Without the ability to subject themselves to a critical reading, arriving at a better understanding of why they think what they think and do what they do, students are condemned to an unexamined life, which Socrates long ago said was not worth living.

One of the best ways to develop a more critical personal literacy is by asking questions. Not just any question will do, however. Students must discover or invent a thoughtful, open-ended "why" question that challenges them, because analysis begins with the question "Why?" This notion puzzles students initially, perhaps because so much of their schooling—including their use of computers and the Internet—has encouraged them to ask only "What?" When asking "What do I need to do to make this software application work?" the questioner invites close-ended inquiry that perpetuates an impoverished, technical definition of computer literacy. However, one opens the inquiry by asking "Why do I need to make this software application work?" allowing for authentic learning to take place. By simply demonstrating the distinction between "what" questions and "why" questions, a good teacher opens the door to analysis rather than summary, an investigation of cause rather than a recitation of symptoms.

■ PERSONAL LITERACY CHALLENGE 1

The Why List

After students understand the distinction between summary and analysis, they are ready to engage in an activity that will awaken their critical thinking and personal literacy skills: the Why List.

What to Do

1. To begin, ask students to think of a Why question that they cannot answer. They should try to make it something substantial, something that they really would like to answer, because it will help them discover what they think and why they think it. Quite often, a social phenomenon or local problem works well for this. For example: "Why do people enjoy violent computer games?" Each student writes three or four Why questions that could serve as a starting point. After they have their questions, ask the students to choose one to investigate more thoroughly. This should be one for which they do not have an answer but that they would like to figure out.

2. Tell students to log on, open a file, and write their own Why List.

3. Have them type the Why question for which they do not have an answer (make sure that it is neither trivial nor absurd). For example, "Why do people enjoy violent computer games?"

4. Ask them to attempt an answer to that question. They are to begin with the word *because* and write a one-phrase response ("Because violent computer games provide an escape from reality").

5. Have them ask the Why question that their Because answer prompts ("Why do violent computer games provide an escape from reality?").

6. Ask them to answer this new question, beginning with the word *because*, and write a one-phrase response ("Because reality is monotonous, and these games are not.").

7. Then, have them ask the Why question that their new answer prompts ("Why is reality monotonous, but not computer games?").

8. Have students continue in this fashion until they have written 10 Why questions and 10 Because responses.

9. When students have finished, have them read through their list and see where it took them. Then, they should write a brief analysis of the list itself. Did the Why List help them answer the initial question, take them further away from it, or simply cause them to spin in circles? Do they see any causal relationships now that they could not see before?

10. When everyone has finished, ask for volunteers to share their Why List.

Expanding the Challenge

As a class, select Why Lists for further examination as a collaborative exercise. Divide the class into pairs, and have the pairings conduct another Why List exercise via synchronous conversation, with one person asking the Why questions and the other responding. When they find the exercise is not taking them any further, ask them to discuss what happened and prepare a brief presentation for the class.

Teacher's Tip

This exercise works especially well in a networked computer lab where students and teachers can review individual files. With practice, this helps students discover the evolution of their thoughts. They may write their lists on word processors and save the file on diskette before posting it to a class discussion forum or mailing list.

■ WHY ASK WHY? INCREASING STUDENT AWARENESS

Asking students to generate their own questions rather than respond to those of a teacher or standardized exam should seem liberating. However, the open-ended inquiry of the Why List may intimidate some students, particularly those who are uncomfortable with ambiguity. In such cases, it helps to present Personal Literacy Challenge 1 as individual brainstorming triggered by the technology of questions. Indeed, it requires a good deal of knowledge and skill to invent a good question. Students are not compelled to reach conclusions and should feel no pressure to arrive at any. However, they need guidance as well as reassurance that what they are doing is "right." If allowed to ask questions without the pressure of a grade or a final destination hanging over them, they may discover that asking why leads on and on, prompting an infinite succession of inquiries, insights, and associations. It is worth asking them where, on examination of the Why List, they would have gotten had they begun by asking "what" instead of "why." With time, they come to realize that What questions lead them to the cul-de-sac of static answers rather than the open road of dynamic, arguable ones.

A few excerpts from student process journals will illustrate the Why List's contributions to a writing process. The present purpose, however, is to examine the way in which the Why List helps students discover ideas, examine their genesis, and acquire the awareness necessary for personal literacy. Certainly, the Why List and student reflections on the exercise could be handwritten and exchanged in a traditional manner. However, networked computers enable exchanges as well as innovations between students and teachers that a conventional approach could not support. For that reason, the following Why Lists were composed with a word processing program and saved in online folders where students kept their process journals.

Generally speaking, students find the Why List usually takes them in one of two directions, either circling their topic or moving away from it as the inquiry progresses. Let us begin by looking at the latter, which illustrates the impact of the Why List on one student's composition process.

Esteban's Why List

The primary appeal of this exercise is its potential for intellectual and personal discovery. If properly engaged, students will go beyond unexamined assumptions. Like a rower paddling with both oars in the water—in this case, both hemispheres of the brain—students embark on an intellectual journey that begins on a familiar riverbank, but explores unfamiliar waters. The following Why List illustrates this type of journey, undertaken by a student named Esteban as part of a literature class. In the first semester, his class had studied a William Wordsworth poem that claims, "The child is father of the man." The following semester, he discovered echoes of the idea in a West African novel. Rather than accept this platitude, however, Esteban chose to investigate it in the following manner:

Q.   Why is the Child supposedly Father of the man?

A.   Because the habits and experiences of childhood shape adults.

Q.   Why can't the adult overcome those habits and experiences?

A.   Because we are all creatures of habit and it takes tremendous will power to overcome those that are ingrained.

Q.   Why don't we have the will power to overcome these?

A.   Because we are weak.

Q.   Why are we so weak when confronting our habits?

A.   Because we are comfortable in our habits, even if they are bad habits.

Q.   Why are bad habits "comfortable?"

A.   Because they are OUR habits.

Q.   Why can't we break OUR habits?

A.   Because we don't want to break them.

Q.   Don't "want" to or "can't?"

A.   Don't want to.

Q.   If we wanted to break them could we?

A.   Yes, though it'd be difficult.

Q.   Why would it be difficult?

A.   Because it threatens us and it could change us.

Q.   Why is change threatening?

A.   Because it could bring the unknown.

Q.   So we prefer the known "evil" rather than the unknown potential evil?

A.   Yes.

Q.   So that's why the Child's the Father of the Man?

WHY ASK WHY? INVITING RESPONSE   ■

Following this exercise, it is important that students take a moment to see where it led them and ponder what it revealed. It is often helpful to have a classmate read and respond to the list. For example, ask students to read a classmate's Why List and respond to it by indicating what interests them and why. They can circle the most interesting question and answer on the list (perhaps the ones they would choose to launch an essay if it were their list). For example, in response to Esteban's list, a reader might select the following pair:

> Q. Why is the Child supposedly Father of the man?
> A. Because we are comfortable in our habits, even if they are bad habits.

This helps the author of the Why List in a number of ways. For one thing, the author sees which questions and answers others value. This furthers the investigation of ideas and encourages the search for an elusive thesis statement and for more satisfying insights. For another, the juxtaposition of a formerly separated question and answer may reveal a causal relationship that the author had not noticed. Following discussion with a peer reviewer, the author of the Why List could be instructed to use either the question that the reviewer selected or another one that the author wishes to explore. That question is used to generate yet another answer, which may provide the kernel of a thesis. The author then refines that statement until it articulates a clear and cogent argument.

In this instance, the essay that evolved from Esteban's Why List, although somewhat flawed, was one of the liveliest and most insightful in the class. What is pleasing for the reader of such an essay is to see how active the writer's mind is while wrestling with the text. Such essays seem to evolve, exploring issues rather than taking them for granted, questioning ideas rather than merely reciting platitudes announced in the first paragraph. When asked what was most helpful in arriving at his thesis, Esteban was quick to cite the Why List. Although there was obviously far more work to be done, the intellectual journey that began by questioning a cliché allowed him to apply new insights to a text written in a different century and continent. Whereas the Why questions led to the analysis of character and setting, What questions would have looked at only the habits of an individual, the symptoms of a behavior rather than its causes. Esteban enjoyed playing with Why questions on the computer because he could continually change directions, erasing a response or considering other possible answers with a keystroke. Consequently, his thesis paragraph revealed a sophisticated analysis, synthesizing literature to arrive at a unique argument:

> "The Child is Father of the Man" wrote William Wordsworth. Indeed, his opinion is reinforced by the character of Ousmane in Mariama Ba's novel, *Scarlet Song*. The Child who would become Ousmane, husband of Mireille, develops habits which will later enslave that man. His habits and reluctance to shed them are essentially responsible for his slavery. Ultimately, one learns from Ousmane that if we do not shed habit, risking change and personal turmoil, we are destined to remain forever controlled by the child within us.

April's Why List

Although it is rewarding to see students put both oars in the water, on some occasions they find their boat spinning in circles because of their obsession with the topic. To extend the metaphor, hanging on to the original question and topic instead of making an intellectual departure is like paddling with one oar in the water and the other in the boat. The following presents a student who was spinning in circles, desperately clinging to the original topic by asking only variations of her original question. After consultation with her teacher, however, she decided to let go and see where the questions would take her. It is worth noting, too, that where Esteban was concerned with the composition of an essay, this student employed the Why

List to examine a complicated text. Notice the evolution of her inquiry and the subsequent amusement in her reflection at where this has led her:

Q.   Why weren't the men's actions controlled in *The Handmaid's Tale?*

A.   Because it was the woman's responsibility.

Q.   Why is it the woman's responsibility?

A.   B/c we were the birthing gender.

Q.   Why does that matter?

A.   B/c men say so.

Q.   Why does it matter that the men say that?

A.   B/c they are the ones in power.

Q.   Why are they in power?

A.   B/c women were taught to be submissive

Q.   Why were women taught to be submissive?

A.   B/c we are the weaker sex

Q.   Why are we the weaker sex?

A.   B/c we are not as physically able as men.

Q.   Why does that play a role in power?

A.   B/c in order to win we have to be strong.

Q.   Why do we have to be strong physically?

A.   B/c war needs us to be.

Q.   Why do we worry about war?

A.   B/c rebellion is constantly around us.

Although this particular list may not accomplish as much as Esteban's, it is an important part of April's thought process. Before she begins to write an essay defending her position, she needs to discover what that position is and why she holds it. The Why List may help her identify assumptions, notice subconscious patterns and connections, and, ultimately, discover questions that inspire further inquiry and deeper understanding of her views. April's reflection takes her beyond superficial concerns and shows her marveling at the distance she has traveled, noting a curious parallel that could plant the seed for her essay:

A brief analysis would lead me to think that I totally went off the subject. I was evaluating the men's actions and their lack of supervision and I ended up with worrying about war. I guess if you think about it the men's actions weren't controlled because they were at war. And in order to win the war their minds have to be free of "inconsequential things" like sexual promiscuity and pregnancy. It's funny how I ended with war and I wasn't even thinking about it. The movie's setting was during a war.

Kara's Why List

April has clearly launched an intellectual journey by liberating herself from the constraints of the initial topic and question. However, not every student writer finds this situation comfortable. In the following example, Kara takes a similar journey. Indeed, the Why List has once again taken on a life of its own, but as the reflection indicates, Kara does not know what to make of this. Is it cause for celebration or consternation?

Q.   Why is modern society transfixed by television?

A.   B/c they like the shows.

Q.   Why do they like the shows?

A.   B/c they're interesting.

Q.   Why are these shows interesting?

A.   B/c they are about human life.

Q.   Why do people want to watch shows about human life?

A.   B/c it inspires them.

Q.   Why does it inspire them?

A.   B/c they think their own lives are boring or lacking excitement.

Q.   Why do they think their lives are boring?

A.   B/c they aren't doing the things on the shows

Q.   Why aren't they doing the things on the shows?

A.   B/c they don't have enough time for them.

Q.   Why don't they have enough time?

A.   B/c they work long hours.

Q.   Why are they working long hours?

A.   B/c they want to earn money.

Q.   Why do they want money?

A.   B/c they want to buy stuff.

Q.   Why do they want stuff?

A.   B/c society says stuff is good.

Kara's Reflection

I don't think my why list went in the direction I wanted it to go—it led to consumerism when I thought it would have led to the dumbing down of society, or something along that line. But I guess if I had answered something differently, it would have gone in that direction—or a totally different direction.

What should the teacher do in cases in which students are spinning in circles or uncertain about the direction in which their thinking has taken them? Teachers must tread carefully, offering guidance and encouragement without doing all the work for a student. This requires a delicate balancing act: on one hand, nurturing, so the student does not lose faith in the enterprise, yet, on the other, demanding intellectual courage. Without striking such a balance, the student could falter and give up hope of discovery. With an excess of attention, however, teachers may interfere with the journey, their desire to help paradoxically hindering the development of the critical-thinking skills necessary for students to acquire personal literacy. This is where networked computers prove an ally, however, providing opportunities for students to collaborate in synchronous discussions during class or asynchronous discussions afterward. As a result, students can continue the Why List in an online writing environment, maintaining focus and energy in an online writing environment in a manner that would be difficult and tedious offline.

CASE STUDY: THE WHY LIST ONLINE   ■

Although one could, of course, have students write the Why List without computers, computers help facilitate not only this exercise but variations and discussions of it. Beyond this lie opportunities for collaboration, including the synchronous discussions introduced in Chapter 3.

In the following example, the teacher arranged a group discussion of Why Lists to inspire open-ended inquiry and introduce students to a new writing environment. Indeed, this transcript is drawn from one group's initiation to synchronous, online discussion. In it, the teacher encourages a movement from broad, general questions that reveal superficial thought toward more specific ones that demand closer examination. Because this was their initiation to a new medium, many of the students found this exercise particularly challenging, but notice how much they accomplish through this telecollaborative effort. Their discussion helps them sort through questions as an online community of inquiry, discovering causal relationships that they had not previously considered. It is these relationships that the teacher hopes will become more apparent, taking the students to a new level of comprehension, a place where they learn something about the world and themselves.

Before proceeding to the transcript, it is worth noting that it presents the most difficult synchronous discussion presented thus far. Given the nature of this communication medium, which allows students to simultaneously type responses and post them to the shared writing space of the synchronized bulletin board, many of the threads seem to cross one another. In other words, one speaker may make a statement that is not addressed until several other speakers have also posted, due to the simultaneity of the composition and serendipity of their postings. This presents challenges for the reader of this text, because it is sometimes difficult to follow a particular thread of the conversation, but this challenge mirrors the one that the participants confronted. Furthermore, because of the limitations of the computer screen, it can be difficult to keep up with messages as they scroll down the screen, pushing their predecessors out of sight above them.

To approximate the experience, imagine that, after 20 lines of text, each subsequent line, which appears at the bottom of the screen, displaces the one at the top. This means students must read quickly, type brief responses, and concentrate on particular threads as they evolve.

Teacher:	I thought we'd use this inaugural Interchange session to discuss the "Why Lists" that you just created in class. Here are a few questions that we can begin with: What was your initial question and where did your "Why List" take you as you proceeded? What, if anything, did the "Why List" help you see in terms of causal relationships that you couldn't see before? Did you find yourself moving further away from your initial question or simply spinning in circles around it? What might you do next to pursue this investigation? OK, so what question would you like to begin with?
Nick W.:	Why do businesses like to take advantage of customers?
Darlene D.:	I asked: Why MLK Blvd has deeper holes than the Grand Canyon?
Brad N.:	I started with the question, "Why is it so hot?"
Brian E.:	I asked "Why are we protecting the Barton Springs Salamander?"
Kelsey M.:	Why do people like to gossip?
Ericka J.:	That's a great question Darlene, my car thinks so too!
Nick W.:	Because our tax money is being wasted.
Andrea T.:	I asked why do so many underage kids abuse drugs and alcohol?
B. J.:	Why are college students now taking so much longer to graduate?
Zach V.:	The why list helped me realize how many factors [there] can be in a simple question
Darlene D.:	Nick, what was your last answer to why businesses take advantages of customers?
Nick W.:	Kids abuse alcohol because they were not raised right.
Teacher:	Was the initial question the most interesting one that you asked?
Tina D.:	My first question was why some people risk their lives by participating in activities such as high-speed rollercoasters or bungee jumping.
Mike S.:	What businesses do you think take advantage?
Brad N.:	I think kids abuse alcohol because they want to get "away"
Kelsey M.:	Andrea, Because it gives them a false sense of being grown-up . . . gives them freedom
Andrea T.:	I thought that kids abuse alcohol because they have low self-esteem
Nick W.:	Every business takes advantage in some way.
Teacher:	. . . or, did you discover a more insightful question further down the list?

Manish C.:	Why is the personal life of a political person such a big deal?
Brad N.:	Advertisers take advantage!!!
Darlene D.:	Nick, that's pretty funny, how did you get to that?
Ericka J.:	Yeah, I think the businesses aimed at youth exploit the most though.
Nick W.:	Because the American public is infatuated with SEX.
Kelsey M.:	I ended up linking gossiping to personal security . . .
Andrea T.:	Tina: what did you put as your first answer?
Mike S.:	I think "taking advantage" is what they feel they need to do to get ahead.
Teacher:	Nick, to whom are you speaking about Sex?
Kelsey M.:	Nick: why does sex sell?
Zach V.:	There were more insightful questions, like why do people want entertainment instead of knowledge
Matt S.:	Andrea, perhaps because it is semi-taboo in our culture. At the same time that authority figures tell them of the terrible evils of drugs and alcohol, their peers likely appear to just be having a good time with it. So, youth just feel misinformed perhaps and want to experiment, at least initially.
Neal R.:	My initial question was "why does it take an average of more that five years to graduate from UT?" The question took me to questions about funding the university. This was quite far away from the initial question. I figured it would not go very far. Next I might look at students' choices that might cause them to stay at UT longer than necessary.
Matt S.:	Knowledge takes work.
Nick W.:	I'm talking to the person who asked about a politician's personal life.
Tina D.:	I found that my question went from being a lighthearted curious one into a deeper self-examining one, if that makes any sense.
Brad N.:	Anyways, I started with Why is it so hot, and ended up with something like Why are there so many people studying research in medicine?
Lisa C.:	People like to gossip negatively because they want to make themselves look good.
Zach V.:	what's so bad about work?
Darlene D.:	Lisa, What's so bad about making yourself want to look good?
Brad N.:	People gossip because they feel bad about themselves some how.
Matt S.:	My question strayed a lot. It started with the relation of rational to intuitive aspects in education and ended up with why people fear death.
Kelsey M.:	Lisa . . . that was my first answer . . .

Mike S.:	Work takes work
Andrea T.:	I finally came up with that the reason kids abuse alcohol is because they have low self-esteem which comes from an unending cycle of bad parenting.
Kelsey M.:	why does sex sell?
Ericka J.:	I found that as I got deeper into asking more questions, I really had no answers . . . they were random guesses.
Manish C.:	I saw that in the end we had to choose that person to make decisions for us and we want him to be more representative of who our ideal person is.
Matt S.: Kelsey:	Because it is interesting and primal?
Teacher:	Tina—how, specifically, did that happen? Were you conscious of it at the time or did it just seem to evolve beyond your control?
Tina D.:	Neal, personally I think it's important to take breaks during one's academic career. Having a little bit of fun complements the hard work that goes with college life.
Nick W.:	Sex sells because people are bored.
B. J.:	My questions became absurd quickly as I asked questions about the workplace and the possibility that if people aren't required to take more classes then we might as well have robots take over our day to day jobs.
Matt S.: Brian:	Ditto. My experimentation was exactly that. What I'd been told via normal courses of education didn't add up to what I was seeing around me.
Neal R.: Tina:	if you were at a private college and had to pay a lot higher tuition, would you have the same opinion?
Lisa C.:	Sex sells because it is a prohibited form of expression—we jump on anything that's taboo, that deviates from the day to day cultural norm of existence.
Manish C.:	I found [myself] moving to another question.
Matt S.:	Tired of not having meaning in their lives? Or at least, not what they perceive as meaning?
Teacher:	If we think of the "Why List" as a process, not a product, then what does it tell us about the process of discovering causal relationships?
Nick W.:	Maybe we all need to release some tension in some way.
Tina D.: Mr. B:	I was conscious of it at the time. It seemed to occur about the 2nd or 3rd question. People looking for thrills, people bored with life, people not happy with decisions in their lives . . .
Brad N.:	I think my questions went too far from my subject
Manish C.:	Ask a new why question with my initial question in mind.
Zach V.:	That causal relationships are complex

As one can see from this brief excerpt (if printed in its entirety, this 10-minute session would continue for another 15 pages), for the most part, these students began with superficial questions and knee-jerk reactions. Like many adolescents, they were more inclined to offer superficial answers than ask questions that would further their inquiry. Some of the questions may not yield thoughtful insights, for they lead to close-ended answers ("Why is it so hot?"). However, one can already see that the collaborative questioning helps individual students dig beneath the surface questions to discover a more challenging line of inquiry. The chances are good that these students will stumble on personal epiphanies, ones that begin with an initiation to the world but may lead to startling self-revelations. Notice, for instance, Zach V.'s discovery: "The why list helped me realize how many factors [there] can be in a simple question." Nevertheless, a flawed question riddled with assumptions gives way to a flawed answer and still more flawed questions. At some point, students need to step back from their Why List and consider alternative answers for a particular question, each of which could inspire a different answer.

PERSONAL LITERACY CHALLENGE 2   ■

The Hypertext Why List

In this challenge, synchronous discussions not only help students develop greater discourse literacy, but also encourage them to explore the ideas generated in their Why Lists to arrive at more satisfying personal literacies. By doing so, students are compelled to question assumptions and dive beneath the surface of their initial questions and answers.

What to Do

1. With the aid of a liquid crystal display panel, have students present their Why Lists to the entire class.

2. As students present their lists, encourage discussion of each list's evolution, and pause to consider alternative questions or answers. Students can quickly demonstrate the thought process involved in the early stages of an inquiry.

3. Following the presentations, arrange the class in small groups to create hypertext Why Lists. This can be done on paper, in a text file, or as a hypertext document (depending on the teacher's comfort level with technology).

4. Each group must generate questions that could potentially invite several responses. Encourage students to write down all the possible answers for each question, then all the possible questions they can think of in response to an answer. Soon, their papers, text files, or hypertext documents will be filled with questions and answers that indicate the exponential growth of questions. Figure 4.2 offers an illustration by starting with a question raised earlier in this chapter.

Figure 4.2   The Hypertext Why List

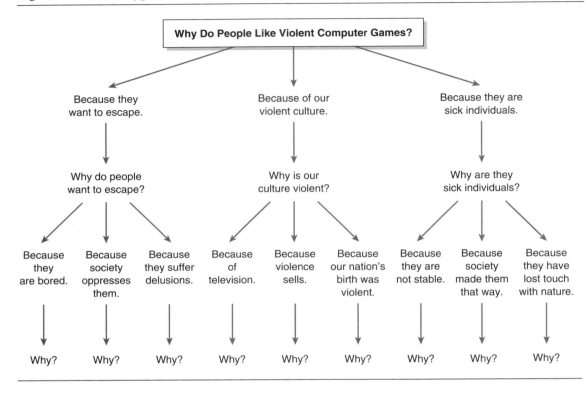

■ BEYOND PERSONAL INQUIRY: COMMUNITY LITERACY

The sequence of challenges in this chapter demonstrates how classroom teachers can use networked computers to help students develop personal literacy skills. The students' composition of the Why List initiated a personal exploration, helping them delve beneath the surface of their assumptions. However, in some instances, they found themselves unable to go beyond certain preconceived notions, their thoughts limited by what they had already embraced as true without understanding why. At that point, they needed to test their ideas in a community, which is what the synchronous, online discussion enabled. Although this encourages a further extension of their ideas and a deeper intellectual odyssey, it may still allow them to neglect certain "blind spots" in their thinking. What if, for instance, their initial question betrays a stubborn assumption, one they cannot perceive because they are too immersed in a culture that accepts the belief ("Why are televisions such a good medium for broadcasting information?"). Worse still, their responses to these assumptions may draw on prejudices that they seldom question because their social milieu does not encourage them to consider alternative viewpoints ("Q: Why is country music so stupid? A. Because only stupid people listen to it."). By employing the Why List in various forms and through various media, teachers can help students move beyond their assumptions to acquire a more satisfying personal literacy.

Indeed, questions are an important technology employed in every class. Too often, however, it is the teacher who generates the questions. By assigning that responsibility to students, however, teachers enable them to acquire more control and ownership of their education. The Why List and the exercises it inspires help students realize the significance of questions, including the way in which particular questions dictate certain answers. This, in turn, teaches them the importance of refining their questioning skills. Ultimately, they cannot ignore the assumptions that their questions and answers rest on. If the teacher explores those assumptions with students as part of an online exercise, it helps them develop a greater awareness of who they are, the ideas that shaped them, and the history of those ideas. Clearly, this is an essential part of the self-discovery required for personal literacy. Also, it serves students well when they enter a community of inquiry where they need to "read" others as well as themselves.

That thought leads to the focus of the next chapter, which asks students to turn attention away from themselves and look outward, acquiring the skills necessary for community literacy.

5

Community Literacy

Composing Ourselves in a Virtual Community

How does one find a niche in a community, contributing to its development while respecting its ethos? How does one learn to "read" a community from afar? The answer to both questions has more to do with personal maturity and initiation—to both the world and the self—than it does with technology. However, by using networked technology, teachers can help students build on the personal literacy skills discussed in Chapter 4, while finding a meaningful place and purpose in an online community (see Figure 5.1).

Figure 5.1

Community Literacy

Community literacy is the ability to engage with "the other," developing mutually beneficial relationships through collaborative endeavors intended to transform an indifferent society into a supportive community.

Prior to the creation of the World Wide Web, champions of virtual community sometimes made it sound as though all one needed to become a member of one was a computer and broadband connection. However, this is akin to saying that all one needs to become a member of a physical community is a street address. In both cases, genuine participation demands far more. Howard Rheingold (1993), an early advocate of virtual community, has observed modern distinctions between community and society while conceding that these terms may not adequately describe what occurs in cyberspace:

> When we say society, we usually mean citizens of cities in entities known as nations. One takes those categories for granted. But the mass-psychological transition that people made to thinking of ourselves as part of modern society and nation-states is historically recent. Could people make the transition from the close collective social groups, the villages and small towns of pre-modern and pre-capitalist Europe, to a new form of social solidarity known as society that transcended and encompassed all previous kinds of human association? Emile Durkheim, one of the founders of sociology, called the pre-modern kind of social group gemeinschaft, which is closer to the English word community, and the new kind of social group gesellschaft, which can be translated roughly as society. All the questions about community in cyberspace point to a similar kind of transition that might be taking place now, for which we have no technical names. (pp. 63–64)

While we may lack terms to describe some of the online transitions and social groups, we clearly attach different meanings and connotations to *society* and *community*. *Society* is the less personal, modern derivative of the romantic *community*. While a public society requires little more than physical existence and common law, a community defines itself through a shared sense of purpose and agreements that hold individuals accountable without necessarily regulating their every action. Societies speak of laws and contracts, but communities rely more on the implicit trust of covenants and individual commitment to the well-being of the group. Consider, for example, how a school community depends on an understanding of the unspoken rules. By the time students reach high school, they have been conditioned to raise their hands when they wish to speak. How did this come about? Where is this rule written? Perhaps it was written on the chalkboard or poster paper in an elementary school classroom, but by the time students reach high school, it is simply understood that this is the way to signal their desire to speak without interrupting someone else. It is a tried-and-true convention that supports turn taking and civil discourse practices that signal respect for others and a commitment to the well-being of the classroom community.

So what are the rules for discourse in an online community of learners? How do participants facilitate discussions to make sure that turn taking occurs and that outspoken students pause to let others speak and reciprocate? How do they develop a sense of community rather than become an indifferent society? This is not merely a matter of semantics. Rather, it speaks to the fundamental concept of sharing something with others, which is implicit in the ideas of "co-mmunication" and "co-llaboration" within a "co-mmunity." Yet, what if there is no shared sense of purpose, no reciprocal correspondence, and no collaborative effort? Can one honestly apply the term *community* in such instances? Would it not be more accurate to think of this as a social group whose members, like suburban households sharing the same Zip code, possess a common trait but not a common purpose or commitment to one another?

In essence, this describes the difference between genuine, reciprocal relationships and dysfunctional ones. Despite the hype that claims the Internet will fulfill the promise of a "global village," reciprocity remains a critical issue in telecollaborative learning activities. Quite often, students become so preoccupied with what they want to say—which manifests itself in an obsession with their postings, their Web pages, and their life— that they forget to think about the concerns of their community. Consequently, they fail to engage with "the other," forfeiting opportunities to develop the mutually beneficial relationships that transform an indifferent society into a supportive community.

How do educators avoid such a sad state of affairs? The next challenge will help students think about their role in an online community. It places turn taking in the foreground, emphasizing not only the participants' need to listen to others, but also building on others' ideas in a truly collaborative manner. Hopefully, it will initiate them to the idea of community literacy and the skills required to achieve it.

COMMUNITY LITERACY CHALLENGE 1 ■

The Sequential Story

The Media Literacy Challenge at the end of Chapter 1 offered an exercise designed to help students think about the impact of writing technology on their writing process. The writing activity at the core of that exercise, which divided the class into small groups, was a "sequential story." Let's return to that exercise now to help develop an online community, engaging students in a telecollaborative writing exercise. Rather than employ a variety of media to compose this story, however, they will conduct all of it through electronic mail.

What to Do

1. Create groups of two to three students.

2. Ask each group to designate a group e-mail address.

3. Create and share with students a "sequence," so that each group knows to whom they should send the narrative when they have finished adding their paragraph.

4. Share the following instructions:

You have been selected to participate in a unique experience that will blend collaborative work, electronic mail, the Internet, and our collective creativity.

Welcome to the Sequential Story!

Here's how it works. Each group will have an opportunity to write one paragraph of a collaborative story about a person in a place with a problem. Your teacher will compose the opening paragraph, which describes the person, place, and problem. When you receive the Sequential Story, read what others have already written. Then compose a paragraph that continues the narrative, and add it to the bottom of the story. Forward your revised version of the story in an e-mail message to the next group on the list, and a send a copy ("cc") to your teacher. To avoid confusion, please do *not* send a "cc" to anyone else. Here is the sequence we'll use:

The Teacher:

1. Group 1:
2. Group 2:
3. Group 3:
4. Group 4:
5. Group 5:
6. Group 6:
7. Group 7:
8. Group 8:
9. Group 9:
10. Group 10:
11. The Teacher: Ultimately, the story will return to your teacher, who has an opportunity to bring the story to a close.

Teacher's Tip

Depending on the size of the class and the ratio of students to computers, divide the group into pairs or trios. Even if there is a 1:1 ratio of students to computers, do this to encourage a collaborative effort. If space allows, trios often work well, allowing one student to sit at the keyboard with partners flanked on either side. For a smaller class, pairs will work, but the more groups there are, the more chances something will go awry.

What Each Group Should Contribute

As we've seen before, stories are usually about a person in a place with a problem. This story is no exception. Describe what happens to the main character when he or she visits your school (or town, neighborhood, or home). One special request: Please conclude your paragraph with a question that our character may ask the next group on the list. When you send the story on, make certain you type in the correct e-mail address to keep the process going.

■ CASE STUDY: A TELECOLLABORATIVE, SEQUENTIAL STORY

There are many ways to build an online community, but a telecollaborative, sequential story proves to be a good starting point. During a World Links for Development (WorLD) seminar, a group of teachers in Uganda used this exercise to compose the story featured in this case study, "Marabou

Michael's Quest." Since the teachers were learning about telecollaboration at a time when their schools lacked Internet connectivity, they created a scenario that closely paralleled their own. The "person in a place with a problem" was Marabou Michael, a teacher who wanted to create an e-mail project for his students but lacked access to the Internet and experience with electronic mail and telecollaborative learning. The respective groups, composed of teachers from 10 different schools in Uganda, were encouraged to offer a brief dialogue Michael might have with one of the teachers involved in the training session or with a school administrator who was working on the creation of the school's network.

As experienced teachers know, it is essential that they modify exercises like this to meet the needs of their students and curriculum. While this scenario might not apply to many cases, it illustrates how online activities can help establish and support collaborative work and a community of learners. The following transcript is the result of a week's effort, in which the sequential story was passed from the workshop leader to the respective groups. As indicated in the instructions, each group added a paragraph to the narrative before passing it along via electronic mail. While they did meet in face-to-face sessions throughout the week, this exercise could have been conducted entirely at a distance. What mattered most, though, was helping the participants gain an understanding of how members of an online community can help one another, working together to construct something in just one week that they would have needed much longer to accomplish alone.

Marabou Michael's Quest

Teacher: It was another rainy afternoon in Jinja. Marabou Michael was restless. He had just finished reading an article in The New Vision that made him anxious. "Innovative Teachers Create E-mail Projects" read the headline. The article described extraordinary projects that these teachers conducted through electronic mail and the Internet to teach their students in Uganda. Marabou Michael, who taught history and geography at Lugazi High School in Jinja, wondered how he might begin to do such things. He had heard from a friend of his that teachers at Mukono Bishop's College had participated in a recent training program. Perhaps they could help him? Yes, perhaps. So he decided to take a journey to ask the teachers at Mukono Bishop's College this question: "What technology would he need in order to participate in such projects?"

Bishop's: At Bishop's Senior School, the teacher, Mr. Kigozi who is in charge of the computer lab advises Michael that he will need the following items: a computer; telephone line; modem; and a room. He is then advised to proceed to Mwiri for more assistance. At Mwiri he asks this question: "How can I integrate this into the school curriculum?"

Mwiri: At Busoga College Mwiri, the deputy headteacher (Daudi M.) and the two teachers who had earlier on attended a WorLD workshop

(Henry M. and Charles K.), advised as follows: the computer had to be a multimedia computer; the telephone line had to be reliable; and they needed a steady and stable power supply. On the question of the curriculum, they did not have all the necessary information and advised that Iganga SS could help out if he asked them: "Which class should I introduce this to? My Western Africa history course or my A-level Land Forms course?"

Iganga: We are planning to run a project on ecology with an A-level class. It is appropriate for us because it requires research and exchange of information with other schools. It does not require any complicated diagrams. As for your case we would advise you to start with African History because it does not require complicated diagrams. For more information we advise you to contact Bukoyo S.S. and ask them: "Which subject do you think is most appropriate?"

Teacher: Apparently, nobody was home at Bukoyo, so Marabou Michael went to Ntare to see if they could answer this question.

Ntare: We think that the most appropriate subject to start with is History. This is because it involves a lot of arguments. If different schools are given questions on different topics, the results would be amazing. However, we are sending you to Bweranyange to ask the following: "How long would you give the different schools to send their feedback? How frequently will they exchange e-mail?"

Bweranyange: We would advise one week for a school to get well researched information. Does Kibuli find this idea practical and beneficial?

Kibuli: On arrival at Kibuli, Michael met Richard who had attended the WorLD Links workshop. He agreed with Bweranyange that one week was actually enough time for research, provided you have partners who are active. Michael was then advised to contact Makerere College to ask: "How should he prepare both teachers and students for the project?"

Makarere: At Makerere College School, Michael had a discussion with the three teachers that attended a WorLD Links Training Workshop. Mr. Darnis K., the coordinator, Mr. Peter D., the Assistant Coordinator, and Mrs. Joy M., the Headmistress, advised him to link up with either St. James SS in Jinja or Namilyango College in Mukono that have the Internet connection to help him train the Resource Teachers. For the training of the students, he was advised to contact Bombo SS. "How should he prepare students for the project? What age group should he begin with?"

Bombo: We in Bombo are not very familiar with such projects. We have just had the training in Internet connection but we are equally interested and we have made a start. We would like to advise you to start with the age group between 14 and 16 that is senior 2 to senior 4 students. This is because they would have been in school long enough. However, Kitante may be able to give you more advice. Ask them this: "How supportive is your headmaster of such projects? What must I do to get support from my headmaster?"

Kitante:	Mr. K, the deputy headteacher in charge of computer studies, informed Mr. Marabou that the headteacher at Kitante Hill School has been very supportive of such projects. It may, however, require some funding from the parents. To get support from him about the advantages of e-mail, he advised Michael to contact Mr. Buddy, the Worldlinks trainer, for more information on how the parents could be convinced to assist.
Teacher:	As a teacher, Marabou Michael, I'm sure you have learned that the best way to persuade parents to do something is through their children. So my advice to you now is to include your students in this community of inquiry. I'm sure they've got a few questions they'd like to ask. So, why not ask them to help you create, develop and sustain an online community? If you build it with them, Michael, I'm fairly certain that their parents will come.

COMMUNITY LITERACY CHALLENGE 2   ■

Putting E-mail Into the Right E-envelope

As the Sequential Story indicates, even the simplest electronic mail activities can inspire enjoyable, educational collaborations. They can do this, that is, if students demonstrate concern for their community, paying close attention to the individuals and logistics that shape its discourse and interactions. It's also worth noting that the training workshop that produced the sequential story of Marabou Michael had several advantages that teachers may not enjoy while facilitating a telecollaborative learning activity. For one thing, all the participants gathered each day for face-to-face discussions. This provided opportunities to clarify the instructions through traditional classroom interactions. The workshop also presented a fairly controlled setting, with all participants using the same hardware and software. Things are seldom this tidy in cyberspace, however. In the real world—beyond training workshops—the conditions will vary, and participants will occasionally misinterpret instructions or neglect them altogether.

This raises an obvious, though persistent, problem: What should the teacher do when an online community breaks down? How do correspondents handle the confusion when misdirected private messages go to the wrong person or, worse still, a public audience? The print equivalent of this is the situation in which an adolescent writes two letters, one to a grandmother and the other to a friend. Both letters describe what happened at the school dance on Friday night. Of course, the recollection of these events (and the vocabulary used to describe them) is dictated by audience as much as by individual writing skills. After writing the two letters and feeling satisfied they will please the respective audiences, the writer makes the mistake of placing them in the wrong envelopes. Thus, an 80-year-old grandmother gets to read about what went on behind the gymnasium Friday night and a 16-year-old friend hears about "all the really nice chaperones."

One must learn to cope with such awkward moments in life. To help prepare for them in cyberspace, this exercise asks students to consider their course of action when the accidental distribution of a private e-mail message through a listserv broadcasts it to a public audience. This presents unique challenges for an online community, especially if its members have not acquired the kind of sophisticated community literacy required to cope with the situation. What should the sender or recipient of publicly distributed private messages do? How does one handle the conflation of public and private messages that blurs former distinctions, revealing private intimacies that embarrass the individual and deliver more (personal) information than the community desires?

What to Do

1. To help think through this matter, have students consider a familiar scenario. Imagine that a bored high school student decides to write a personal e-mail message at the end of a class session and send it to a distant peer that she met through a telecollaborative learning activity their teachers had arranged.

2. Share the following message and scenario with students:

The Message

> Hi! I've like finished all my work for this class so I'm gonna use the rest of the time to send you e-mail. This project's kinda cool but it's a lotta work. I wish we could just send fun messages like this instead of doing all that BORING research. Our teacher gets hysterical if we don't find like the best stuff, ya know? After awhile I'm like, omigod, who cares? I don't know about you but my brain aches after searching through all those Web sites trying to find something on our topic. But that's not what I want to talk about. I wanted to tell you about this really cute guy in our class. He's soooo HOT! And nice, too. I've been like flirting with him for the past week and I think he kinda likes me too. I hope so 'cuz he's sooooo HOT! oops, outta time. I'll tell ya more about him manana. ciao 4 now!

The Scenario

Imagine that instead of sending this message to a private e-mail address, as the author intended, that it was accidentally forwarded to a listserv that automatically distributed it to an online community's mailing list. Embarrassing, right? Common, too. So, what's the proper thing to do when you're either the author of such a misdirected message or an unintended recipient? Think about this for a moment. Re-read the message. Then, proceed to the next step: the questions.

3. Ask students to use a notebook to write out their thoughts for two viewpoints before proceeding to the consequences for the recipient

and author of a private e-mail message placed in a public "envelope." Tell them to be honest and to think carefully about the problem, trying to imagine the potential consequences for each response before advancing to the discussion of them. After all, they'll soon need to make their own judgments in these matters, so it's a good idea to develop their community literacy skills in anticipation of such awkward moments.

4. Share this viewpoint with students:

Viewpoint for Recipients of the Message

What should you do if you're an accidental recipient of a private message? There are many possibilities, but the following are perhaps the most common. In your notebook, jot down what you think about each of these possible reactions, then choose the one that you prefer and be prepared to explain why.

    a. Ignore the message.
    b. Forward the message to others.
    c. Send a private message to the sender.
    d. Send a public message to the listserv (i.e., mailing list).

After they've finished writing and thinking about these options, ask students to take a few minutes to discuss them with their classmates in small groups. When all the groups have finished, ask for a "reporter" to summarize responses from each group. It is best to discuss the responses prior to reading the "consequences for the recipient," since students will have an opportunity to reach their own conclusions before considering someone else's viewpoint. What's more, they may find that their conclusions, or those of their classmates, are more satisfying in the context of their school and community. When the groups are done discussing their own conclusions, discuss the following consequences with them.

Consequences for the Recipient

What should you do if you're an accidental recipient of a private message? Whether you like it or not, your participation in this community of learners requires that you take responsibility for its care and development. What you've just encountered is a message that conflates computer literacy, civil literacy, discourse literacy, personal literacy, and, now, community literacy. What you do, or don't do, will affect everyone in this online community. So it's wise to give this some careful thought before you react. In fact, more often than not, an impulsive reaction to a "public e-mail message" causes more problems than it solves. So let's approach this one with a clear head as we consider some alternative approaches.

a. Ignore the message. In many instances, this may be the best course of action, particularly if you don't know the author. Why? Well, there's a good chance the author will hear from several other people who do know her. For now, rather than overreact, it might be best to view this as an honest mistake. However, if the same author should repeat this error, consider option c or d.

b. Forward the message to others. Not a good idea! In fact, it's probably the worst possible response. Not only are you subjecting the author to further embarrassment, but you're invading privacy and getting cheap thrills out of it. This doesn't speak highly of your ethics. If the author discovers that you have had fun at her expense, making her a subject of ridicule, you can expect similar treatment down the road. Do you really want to set this precedent? Do you really want to create that kind of online community?

c. Send a private message to the sender. If you know the author, this may be the best course of action. After all, the author may not be aware of the mistake. More than likely, this private message went public because the author responded to a message she received through a mailing list, hastily pressing the "reply" button rather than typing her counterpart's personal e-mail address. It's a good idea to break this news gently. You're dealing with someone's feelings, and the shock of this news will likely upset this person. If you don't know the author very well, you might contact someone who does or preface your message by saying, "I was just wondering, did you mean to send that message to everyone?" A question like that is often the best rhetorical approach you can take, because it helps the author see the error without rubbing her nose in it. It also suggests that you are a responsible member of this online community.

d. Send a public message to the listserv. This is not the best option, but if you reach for it, be sure to speak in general terms, perhaps as a reminder that the mailing list is reserved for public messages. Just tread carefully. The author is probably embarrassed by the mistake and doesn't need further humiliation. Unless you're looking for enemies, don't single the author out personally; make this a general statement addressing the full community.

   5.   Share the second viewpoint with students:

Viewpoint for the Author of the Message

What should you do if you accidentally send a private message to a public mailing list? In your notebook, jot down your thoughts on each of these possible reactions, then choose one that you would follow and be prepared to explain why.
   a. Pretend it didn't happen, and forget about it.
   b. Send an apology to the mailing list.
   c. Change your name and move to another state.

After students have committed their thoughts to writing, ask if they are prepared to explain why they would choose one of these options. If so, take a few minutes to discuss this in small groups. See if they can reach a consensus, creating guidelines—general agreements or principles, not necessarily laws—for their online community. Afterward, please discuss these "consequences for the author" with the students.

Consequences for the Author

What should you do if you accidentally send a private message of this kind to a public mailing list? Here's one way to think about this: What if it had happened in a face-to-face discussion in class or in an even larger meeting? If you made a mistake, saying something you really shouldn't have—what should you do? Pretend you didn't say it? Apologize? Flee from the room? Perhaps it's not so strange to discover that this situation parallels your predicament in this online community. The difference, of course, is that no one can see you blushing. However, this leads to new temptations, ones that can prove harmful to the community as a whole. Let's take a brief look, then, at the alternatives we've sketched out.

a. Pretend it didn't happen, and forget about it. This is definitely not a good idea. Ignoring a problem seldom makes it go away. More than likely, there are some confused readers out there right now. They haven't a clue what this message is about or why they received it. Don't you owe them an apology? And even if you wish to forget it, don't think for a moment that others will let you. At some point, you're going to have to deal with this. In fact, the moderator of the mailing list will more than likely contact you very shortly to remind you of the distinction between personal and public messages, or perhaps someone else will ask if you meant to send that gem to everyone. Why wait for them to tell you what your conscience has already said? Which brings us to the second option.

b. Send an apology to the mailing list. It takes courage and integrity, but most subscribers will understand, forgive, and respect someone who admits the error of their ways—provided, of course, that this doesn't become a habit! Your apology doesn't need to be more than a sentence ("My apologies for sending the previous message to the mailing list"). However, it establishes you as a responsible member of this online community. Learn from the mistake, and take more care before pressing that "send" button in the future!

c. Change your name and move to another state. Yes, of course it's tempting, but resist the temptation! We're human, after all. We make mistakes. Logging on with a new user name or dropping out of the discussion tells the rest of the community that you're irresponsible. They'll have far more respect if you swallow your pride, admit you made a mistake, and learn from the experience. And while you're at it, remember this experience when you see a "newbie" commit a similar mistake in the future!

COURSE WEB SITES: A COMMUNITY WORK IN PROGRESS ■

Although it may read like fiction, the episode depicted in the preceding challenge remains a common occurrence in online communities. With each new instance, participants encounter difficult questions that merit attention.

How, for example, might one prepare for such events—or at least anticipate them? How does one learn to "read" an online community? What rules and regulations guide these communities? Much of this depends on the purpose of the community and on one's place in it. However, the preceding episode inspires three bits of advice that are worth sharing with students prior to their initiation to an online community:

1. Read the community's mission statement and guidelines for participants.

2. Contact the moderator of the community's mailing list if you cannot locate a mission statement or guidelines. Ask about protocol and the rules and regulations.

3. "Lurk" before you leap! This applies to participation in message boards, newsgroups, mailing lists, chat rooms, blogs, and more. Students should familiarize themselves with the discourse practices in the community and wait for an appropriate moment to introduce themselves as a new member, ask a question, or respond to a discussion thread.

The creation of a class Web site, an increasingly common classroom activity, could be used to reinforce this counsel. Web site construction serves a number of purposes, provided educators approach it as a collaborative work in progress rather than an individual undertaking at the culmination of a project or course. Unfortunately, a common misconception leads the novice to think of a class Web site solely as a product constructed on completion of a particular project. This can be especially problematic if students—or teachers—work in isolation, creating "digital walls" that are stitched together by hyperlinks at the project's end. Fortunately, new software applications have made it fairly easy to assemble a basic Web site without having to learn the tags that Webmasters have used to write hypertext markup language. As a result, it is now realistic for teachers to introduce this as a class project to develop community literacy skills. In fact, if educators think of the class Web site as a collaborative work in progress—and an opportunity to practice what they so often preach about the writing process—they can build the site as both an archive and a medium for communication, the former showcasing course assignments and student work and the latter providing interactive writing spaces.

The particulars of a class Web site are left to the imagination and technical skills of the teacher and students engaged in this activity. Rather than stress the technical aspects, it's important that teachers approach this as an opportunity to develop student literacy skills. Much of what has already been discussed—including media literacy, civil literacy, discourse literacy, personal literacy, and community literacy—will apply to this enterprise. What matters most, however, is making certain that students have a genuine sense of ownership, approaching this not as something they must do to satisfy an assignment, but as a cooperative venture. If students and teachers build it together, collaborating in the design, implementation, and maintenance of the site, they can accomplish far more than they would in isolation. Also, this endeavor requires problem-solving skills and a holistic approach that one could not achieve through disparate exercises.

Ultimately, the Web site as a collaborative work in progress is both a creation and reflection of a particular community of learners. It reinforces the notion of community literacy because each individual must consider his or her contribution to the group effort. Students could work in small groups, developing particular sections, but this still requires an understanding of the overarching purpose of the site—the "argument" that the site as a whole wishes to present. Beyond this, the moment they link from a class Web site to an external site, they connect to another member of the Internet community. This is both exciting and problematic, for it will challenge the teacher and students to stretch their literacy skills. How so? Well, if students lack the critical literacy necessary to distinguish good resources from mediocre ones, imagine how readily they might link to random sources without careful scrutiny.

Every link contributes to the ethos of a Web site, but this is difficult to impress on students who lack the critical literacy necessary to distinguish reliable sources from unreliable ones. Chapter 6 discusses how the pathos of fascinating visual images can overwhelm a student's judgment of the content's logos and the creator's ethos. As a result, they may fail to exercise the critical acumen necessary to make good choices or present a clear, coherent argument through the combination of words and images. For that reason, it is best to begin by stressing the sense of community behind a Web page, focusing on both its form and function, while enabling individual students to learn how each part relates to the whole.

VISUAL LITERACY ■

Although the next chapter focuses on visual literacy, it will draw on an understanding of community literacy to help one think about Web sites as a process rather than a product. As indicated, Web sites are both the creation and reflection of a community of learners. They may begin as collaborative efforts to synthesize texts, images, and sounds, but they become telecollaborative the moment one contributes to them at a distance or establishes hypertext links to neighboring Web sites. By understanding the previous types of literacy—media literacy, civil literacy, discourse literacy, personal literacy, and community literacy—students can now apply a healthier critical literacy to their reading of Web sites. Because many authors—and readers—of Web sites pay so much attention to "cool" graphics, Chapter 6 will approach these creations through the filter of visual literacy. However, it shall examine these visual effects as an expression of a community's image of itself and its purpose. Thus, community literacy skills, which students acquired and refined in this chapter, must now meet the challenges of visual literacy.

6

Visual Literacy

Web Sites, Rhetorically Speaking

I n the beginning, there is the Image.

Before children learn to make words, they must rely on physical images to indicate objects of desire. Infants cannot articulate ideas, for they lack the vocabulary to give them expression, but physical images signify a visual world and introduce them to one of the most basic literacies. Nonetheless, one soon wishes to overcome the limitations of a functional visual literacy, for the ability to see does not necessarily confer the ability to interpret images. Just as the ability to sound letters and form words provides only the most rudimentary reading skills, so the ability to see leaves a person short of the critical visual literacy one must achieve to interpret and understand the visual cues of one's world (see Figure 6.1).

Figure 6.1

Visual Literacy

Visual literacy is the ability to read, interpret, and understand what one sees based on careful examination of the nature and context of the images one encounters.

In *Ways of Seeing,* John Berger (1972) describes this as a strained relationship between knowledge and vision, one which is at once unresolved and symbiotic:

> It is seeing which establishes our place in the surrounding world; we explain that world with words, but words can never undo the fact that we are surrounded by it. The relation between what we see and what we know is never settled. Each evening we see the sun set. We know that the earth is turning away from it. Yet the knowledge, the explanation, never quite fits the sight. . . . The way we see things is affected by what we know or what we believe. (pp. 7–8)

With the advent of the World Wide Web and "graphical interface browsers" (in other words, software that allows one to see images and text), online readers entered a virtual world that presented challenges similar to what Berger (1972) describes here. The Web constructs another world of images and text, and first encounters with it may force one to "explain that world with words, but words can never undo the fact that we are surrounded by it" (pp. 7–8). Indeed, as readers broaden their online bandwidth (the speed at which information may pass through the network), they invite more complex imagery, incorporating sound and motion pictures to create an elaborate text that presents new challenges to their literacy skills. For many students, "coolness" remains the principal criterion for their evaluation of Web sites, which betrays weak literacy skills. By its nature, this coolness is a superficial concern, one that reveals the intimate relationship "between what we see and what we know" (Berger, 1972, p. 7). This concern cries out for development of visual literacy, demanding an improved ability to read and interpret what we see on the Web. This, once again, requires critical literacy, acknowledging that one's vision "is affected by what we know or what we believe" (Berger, 1972, p. 8). Without careful examination of their context and deeper understanding of their nature, one may fail to recognize or interpret significant visual cues on the Web, while imagining things that are simply not there.

■ WHAT ARE YOU LOOKING AT?

How might educators stimulate their students' critical literacy through the development of more astute visual literacy? Once again, this calls for rhetorical analysis. By employing the rhetorical triangle to evaluate Web documents, students can overcome a flawed obsession with cool graphics, which often distracts them from flaws in the documents themselves. They might begin with three fundamental questions when they encounter a Web document:

- *Ethos*: What individual, organization, or institution created this document?
- *Logos*: What argument does this document make, and is it a logical, coherent one?
- *Pathos*: How does this document attempt to persuade its readers through emotional appeals (visual, aural, or textual)?

The teacher may wish to take a more prescriptive stance, requiring attention to these three essential topics as well as a strict sequence. There's good reason to begin with ethos, testing the credibility of a source before examining the quality of its content (logos). Furthermore, it is wise to investigate logos before turning to the pathos of imagery. As the following case study reveals, this line of inquiry compels attention to matters that might otherwise be forgotten, particularly if the seductions of pathos should overwhelm a student's judgment.

CASE STUDY: THE STATE OF *THE ONION* ■

Mr. Bellamy, the instructor of a rhetoric and composition seminar for undergraduates, had repeatedly admonished his charges to pay close attention to sources they selected from the Internet. All too often, he thought, students would browse the Web looking for something cool to put into their essays without considering the source of the information they borrowed. To exacerbate matters, they often failed to provide proper documentation, revealing a scholarly approach that was as casual as it was careless. In the most celebrated instance, one student's citation for a Web site said nothing more than "Internet." Now, as his students prepared for their final essay of the semester, a proposal argument, Mr. Bellamy felt obliged to teach them a lesson in a most unusual manner: He would pull an April Fools' Day prank.

If successful, it would teach his students the value of visual literacy and the dangers of virtual gullibility. More than anything, he wanted to teach them how to read a Web document with a more critical eye, examining information through the filters of ethos, logos, and pathos. By now, they knew enough about the rhetorical triangle to apply it to written words. They seemed quite capable of analyzing newspaper editorials and short essays that had served as the topic of class discussions. However, something happened when they turned to online sources featuring colorful graphics, animated icons, motion pictures, and sound. To practice what he preached as a composition teacher—"show, don't tell"—Mr. Bellamy wondered how he might demonstrate the consequences of weak visual and textual literacy skills. He wanted to present his students with a document that looked real, and even sounded real, but came from an unreliable source or delivered misinformation.

So he went online and used a search engine to locate satirical Web sites. He didn't know where to begin, because he had never before looked for online, satirical publications. He was surprised to find so many but finally settled on an article in *The Onion*, a weekly publication that specializes in satire (http://www.theonion.com). The article, "America Online to Build Three Million Home Pages for the Homeless," claimed that one of the largest Internet service providers in the United States had announced ambitious plans for a unique social service. Beneath its bold headline (see Figure 6.2), the article featured America Online's (AOL's) logo; a picture of Steve Case, the chief executive officer of AOL; and the image of a homeless man pushing a shopping cart full of belongings through snowy streets. Among other things, the article claimed that Mr. Case said "there is room enough for everyone in cyberspace," and that this new program was inspired by the belief that "no American should be without an address."

96

Figure 6.2   *The Onion* Article

America Online To Build Three Million Home Pages For The Homeless

VIENNA, VA—America Online announced Monday that it will do its part in the fight against U.S. homelessness by constructing three million World Wide Web home pages for the nation's homeless citizens.

"In this, the richest nation on earth, no one should have to know the pain of being without a home," said AOL president and CEO Steve Case, announcing the home-pages-for-the-homeless plan. "That's why we're working to make sure that all Americans have a place to call their own."

"There is room enough for everyone in cyberspace," Case said.

Beginning next week, the popular online service will give every homeless citizen his or her own home page, training in the basics of HTML coding, and 512K of storage space.

Homeless persons will also be able to go to their city's Department of Social Services, where a web-trained social worker will help them choose a background color or pattern for their page, assist them in selecting their "hot links" list, and give them a choice of cartoon characters to greet visitors to the page.

"All human beings need a place where they can be themselves, where they can express themselves," Case said. "And that is precisely what a home page provides. Give a person a home page, and you have given that person dignity."

"Like anybody else, homeless people just want a chance," Case continued. "And AOL is giving them just that—a chance to earn prize tokens by playing Zealot trivia. Whether they ally themselves with the Drakulian Empire or the Zsiverian Collective, the nation's homeless will be able to test their sci-fi know-how in a multiple-choice celestial showdown for valuable prizes."

"Keyword: Z," Case said.

Homeless citizens who have severe physical or mental disabilities, Case said, will also be eligible for special "page perks," such as a Java applet of a DOOM cyberdemon or a downloadable list of 100 humorous ways to phone in a pizza order. By early 1999, AOL will also begin offering such persons a "Cartoon Laws Of Physics" text file.

"It is shameful that in America in 1998, with all the wealth and technology we have at our disposal, there are still people out there who have no place to go," Case said. "No American should be without an address."

AOL

One of the millions of U.S. homeless.

AOL president and CEO Steve Case.

Mr. Bellamy liked this very much. It was just believable enough to fool gullible readers. The bold headlines, standard journalistic features, and details of the bogus social program established enough ethos to persuade some students that this was an authentic report; the photos of a smiling Steve Case and the man with his shopping cart would capture them through the emotional appeal of pathos; finally, the argument, though clearly flawed, was just persuasive enough to make less-critical readers think it a sensible proposal. Would his students see right through this, or would they fall into this satirical web of deceit? Would the seductions of visual imagery overwhelm their ability to critique faulty logic ("Give a person a homepage, and you have given that person dignity")? Would they notice how this satire played with words, combining the ideas of a "home" and an "address" to create its humor? Mr. Bellamy honestly wasn't sure what would happen, but he decided to give this a try, typing up a brief prompt for an online discussion, one that would help show students what he had tried to tell them throughout the semester.

On April Fools' Day, Mr. Bellamy greeted his students as he would any other day, then announced that he wanted to hold a synchronous, online discussion to examine a proposal argument in preparation for the final essay assignment of the semester. The focus of the discussion would be a proposal he had discovered while reading an online article. He then divided the class of 21 students into three discussion groups, with students numbering off so that the members of the respective groups were not seated beside each other. Students were given 5 minutes to individually read and study the one-page article on the Internet. They were not allowed to discuss it with their classmates before joining their online groups, which would have approximately 10 minutes for their synchronized discussion.

Much to his delight, the groups conducted an extremely animated debate over this proposal. In fact, it was one of the liveliest synchronous, online discussions Mr. Bellamy had ever witnessed. Despite a deliberate prompt, however, the students failed to consider all three points of the rhetorical triangle. To his amazement and alarm, he watched 21 of 22 students fall victim to the prank, engaging in a heated argument over this most foolish proposal. Not until Mr. Bellamy interrupted to ask a question about ethos did 1 student out of 22 pause to consider the source of the information. What follows is an excerpt from the transcript of one of these small-group sessions.

April Fools: Homepages for the Homeless

Mr. B.:   Let's subject the electronic document that you just read to some rhetorical analysis. Here are a few questions to consider:

—Ethos—How does this electronic document establish its "ethos"? Who is its author? Who is responsible for its publication? What type of article is it?

—Logos—What do you think of the "logos" of this document? What are the warrants behind the argument it presents?

—Pathos—Where do you see evidence of "pathos" in this document? How is it used? Ultimately, how effective is this document? Is it persuasive? Why/why not?

Beth:	I think there is a problem with the logos in the article.
Ally:	I would like to know how many homeless people really want their own Web site and how many of them would rather have that money put into shelters or public housing.
John:	It sounds to me like the guy is trying to build his and the [company's] ethos. The whole idea seems a bit outrageous, a homepage doesn't eliminate homelessness. I think giving a homeless person a homepage will do nothing to better his life. Once he leaves the computer center he [will] still be homeless.
Maya:	I agree, I don't see how it will help the overall homeless problem in our country.
Beth:	The article assumes that a web site is a home.
Linda:	logos—By giving the homeless a webpage, the pain of being homeless is cured? That sounds absurd.
Duane:	I agree with y'all, this idea is pretty lame...he's just trying to make his company sound good, establish his ethos.
Maya:	I guess it may give these people something to do and maybe that will ultimately get them motivated to do something, but directly I don't see a correlation
Ally:	The whole subject seems really absurd to me. Apparently Mr. Case needed something to make him feel a little better about himself, like he was making some BIG contribution to society. HA HA HA
Duane:	I mean what can a homeless person put on his web page?? And how many do u actually think is going to waste their time to go to a shelter and mess with the computers.
Maya:	I THINK MR. Steve Case, has nothing better to do with all his money than to make it seem as if AOL is helping world problems
Beth:	Homeless people aren't going to have easy access to a computer. The money for the computers should go to basic living needs.
Maya:	I agree Duane, I doubt half of those people can read
Maria:	Mr. Case needs to worry about feeding these people if he wants to help. A web address is not going to feed them.
Maria:	His intentions are very questionable. He just wants to make AOL more marketable.
Duane:	Yeah I think he should just donate those money to the charity or something, instead of wasting time and money on this idea.
Beth:	If they can't read, there is no way that they will be able to understand the internet.
John:	I think it will just give them something to do for a good hour a day to take their minds off of their life style. But ultimately they are going to get bored with it after they have put all they can on the web site.
Ally:	I just finished reading this John Grisham novel about homeless people and never realized how overlooked they are by the government

and everyone else, so reading about AOL's little contribution to the poorest of the poor really sets me off.

Duane: I agree with John

Mr. B.:   I agree with many of your points about the issue raised in this piece, but have you considered the source? Who was the author? Where was this published? How would you evaluate its ethos?

Beth: I think AOL wants to improve their image. The article makes it seem like they are doing something that will save all homeless people.

John: That is a big assumption saying that the majority of homeless people can not read, I don't think right now we can really tell how many of them are really illiterate or not.

Maria: Then again, even if Mr. Case's intentions are self-centered, the project might actually result in something positive. The homeless may become motivated, and by creating their own Web site they can learn a lot. Maybe they'll even find a job or want to find a job.

Maria: I agree with Beth.

Maya: Sorry I'm sounding so cynical, but I really don't see a point in making computers and technology accessible to homeless people who do absolutely nothing. . . . If Steve Case really wants to add to logos, why not provide jobs with all the money he has to help the homeless

Duane: Well his ethos is good, I mean he is the president and the CEO, so many people will think that he's trying to help but really he's trying to gain ethos for AOL.

Maya: true

Maria: Who wrote this article? Onion, Inc. Is this all a joke?

Beth: AOL has had some problems in the past that hurt their ethos. Maybe this is a way to build it back.

Linda: But is there any harm with what he's doing?

Duane: is this how we're suppose to evaluate a web page? Because I'm confused about how we're suppose to do out assignment.

Duane: our

Maria: How accurate is the article? Did Mr. Case really say all this? The site doesn't even say who wrote it.

Ally: The article is a big SATIRE!!!!

Maya: In his quotes, Steve Case is sucking up major pathos, probably because he can't depend on his logic to gain support

Maria: Is Onion, Inc. like the *National Inquirer*?

Ally: Look at the bottom of it. It's just a made up story to try to get people to think.

Linda:	ya, it's pretty absurd, maybe it is a joke.
Maya:	What!!!!!!!!!
Ally:	Fiction!!
Maya:	Roger That Ally
John:	I don't think it will motivate them to get a job. I really think it will just side track them and help them put aside for a few minutes the fact that they don't have a job. It will just entertain them so they don't have to deal with not having a job.
Maya:	Don't Agree.
Ally:	Can you believe just how irate we became over something that was not even true?
Maria:	What it says doesn't matter. We can't believe every thing we read. It's off the Internet. We have to be careful.
Duane:	I think this is all just a waste of time, Case has too much time and money on his hand, so he just want to try to establish some ethos for his company.

Student Reflections

What did the students learn from this exercise? Following the synchronous discussions and the revelation that this had been an April Fools' prank, Mr. Bellamy asked each student to read the transcript of the synchronous discussions, which he posted on the class Web site, and then type a brief reflection on what caused them to fall for this foolish prank. In the first of these, Jennifer B. offers one of the most common reactions, lamenting her failure to consider the source and pay attention to the ethos of the Web document:

> I fell for this April Fool's trick because I assumed it was from a legitimate source. Being in a classroom setting, I did not think that the exercise would be fake. I was concentrating more on the assignment than I was on the source. In reading the Interchange that took place after reading the article, I noticed only one person in the classroom said anything about *The Onion* as the source. Even after it was posted that the document was fake, no one responded. It was as if no one cared and that they were more concerned with the other aspects of the exercise. I fell into the same trap as the rest of the class. It has taught the class and myself to always begin with the legitimacy of the source.

Jennifer B.'s comments reveal a disturbing tendency, which one might describe as the "transferal of ethos" from one source to another. In this instance, Jennifer and her classmates transferred the teacher's ethos, and their expectations for the kind of article their teacher would choose, to the

Web document they encountered. Based on informal surveys of students, this seems a common phenomenon. In the following reflection, Brent S. reinforces this notion. He explains his misreading as a consequence of blind faith in the professor and susceptibility to the pathos of the text and images he encountered, which resulted from a preoccupation with the article's appearance:

> Why did I fall for this article? Well, first of all, I guess I believed it because Mr. B. told us to read it. It was something he had found and gave to us. That gave it some credibility in my mind. I thought, "Well, Mr. B. gave it to us, it's most likely not a joke." Why would he give us something to discuss if it weren't real? Now I know why he did it, but that is the main reason why I thought it was real. I also believed it because it looked real. It looked like any other article you would find in an on-line newspaper. It had pictures. It just looked authentic. This experience has hopefully taught me to be more critical of the things I read, especially when they are on the Internet.

There is also the matter of the message. Where the first two reactions stress ethos and pathos, Kara W.'s reflection touches the third point on the rhetorical triangle. She notes the way in which preoccupation with an item's logos—and the heated debates it inspires—can blunt one's attention to other points on the triangle:

> I bought into the article simply because I did not check out the source or author. In fact, it seems that the entire group focused on the logos of his argument, and a little on the pathos. But no one gave a single thought on his ethos. We all overlooked the fact that there was no author, no credentials, and no justification as to why this guy has any authority to write the article. Strange, seeing as how this class emphasizes all THREE parts of the rhetorical triangle, and we managed to totally ignore one. In the future, we must all be more wary of where the information is coming from.

Obviously, statements like these are cause for hope, suggesting that this student has learned a valuable lesson about the rhetorical analysis of Web sites. As this final reflection indicates, an exercise such as this helps students learn a good deal about visual literacy and their own skills. Kelly, the author of the following reflection, had already created her own Web pages and used the Internet extensively for research, yet she couldn't resist the seductions of this satirical presentation. Rather than attempt to explain or excuse her misreading of the document, she seizes this opportunity to look at her own mistakes and learn from them. Much to her credit, she draws valuable lessons from the exercise, recognizing her own tendencies and realizing the actions she must take to prevent future misunderstandings:

It is interesting to see the discussion others had about the subject. It seems I was not the only one who was duped into thinking AOL was actually going to implement this program. It just shows how people are incredibly vulnerable. It is a little bit scary to think that I can be tricked so easily. This was a harmless joke, but if I believe everything I read than I could be giving people false information and perhaps harming myself and others. In the future, I need to look at the source more carefully. If I would have just looked at the address I would have seen that this did not come from AOL. It is important to examine the address. Who is writing it? Why are they writing it? What audience are they writing to? And what message are they trying to portray? These are some of the questions I need to start asking myself instead of immediately divulging into the article.

■ SEEING IS BELIEVING (AND OTHER SATIRICAL LESSONS)

There are many lessons to be learned from this exercise, but perhaps one of the most important echoes John Berger's (1972) earlier observation: "The way we see things is affected by what we know or what we believe" (p. 8). These students, who in many ways are fairly typical undergraduates at a public university, fell for this prank because of what their eyes told them they were seeing. Aesthetically, this item looked like something they might find in the online version of a newspaper or magazine. The bold font style, the color photos, and the AOL logo made them believe they were looking at an authentic document. However, the key to this exercise, and one that Mr. Bellamy understood intuitively, is the manner in which the item is presented. Had the teacher prefaced the exercise by saying, "I thought we'd have some fun on April Fools' Day by looking at some satirical Web sites," students would have brought that expectation—that "belief system"—to their reading of the document. However, since the teacher tied the exercise to the students' assignment—a proposal argument—they brought different expectations with them, expectations that influenced what they saw and how they interpreted it. This speaks volumes about the importance of teaching visual literacy skills. Although educators may not think in these terms yet, the exponential growth of the World Wide Web and Internet connectivity in schools compels them to find ways to teach visual literacy. Exercises like Mr. Bellamy's may help students resist the seductions of fancy graphics and overcome the visual cues that excite the passion of pathos and overwhelm judgment of the author's credibility and logos.

■ MEASURING THE SUM OF A WEB SITE'S PARTS

Teacher's Tip

While some teachers may feel conflicted about deceiving students in this manner, since

In Mr. Bellamy's case, one can see how the use of computer technology assisted him in teaching his students about visual literacy. Students began by reading an online publication, then conducted an online synchronous discussion before they reviewed the transcripts published on the class

Web site. They then wrote a reflection that would appear in their online portfolios. Obviously, this requires a sophisticated level of technology integration, but as schools gain Internet access and teachers devise new ways to employ technology for teaching literacy, learning activities like Mr. Bellamy's could become fairly common. Nevertheless, teachers need a strategy for improving students' critical reading of Web sites, one that calls attention to the seduction of cool graphics, the weakness of poor logic, and the importance of an author's credibility. This is a complex challenge, certainly, for it requires a rhetorical analysis of Web sites that argues for a much more sophisticated visual literacy.

Once again, it's important to distinguish parts from the whole. In the previous exercise, students focused on a Web document, which could be an essay, song, movie clip, or any other item presented on a Web page. To succeed, Mr. Bellamy's students needed to examine the Web page as a whole, understanding its context and purpose. Instead, they chose to treat it as an isolated page, neglecting its hyperlinks to other online documents within *The Onion's* Web site. If they had taken that step, their analysis of the individual document would have led them to inquiries about the electronic publication in which it appeared as well as its creator's purpose. Clearly, this is a complicated process, placing rather extraordinary demands on a reader, but unless students make such an effort, their visual literacy skills will remain stunted, achieving a functional literacy, but not a critical one.

the relationship between student and teacher depends on trust, failure to provide an exercise of this kind could leave students susceptible to the rhetoric of Web documents. "What am I looking at?" should be the first question one asks about Web documents, which is precisely what this exercise teaches students to do. To replicate this exercise, select a satirical article or parody from an online publication. If one chooses a well-known publication such as *The Onion*, make sure the hyperlink takes the group directly to a document buried deep in the pages of this Web site. This will force students to seek background information rather than having it handed to them on the homepage.

VISUAL LITERACY CHALLENGE 1   ■

The Rhetorical Analysis of Web Documents

To model the evaluation process, the teacher may wish to have each student evaluate the same Web document the first time. Subsequent exercises might allow students to look at a Web site of their own choosing.

What to Do

1. Ask students to evaluate a Web document chosen by the teacher.

2. Before distributing the evaluation form, discuss the distinctions between a Web document, a Web page, and a Web site. In Mr. Bellamy's case, he asked his students to evaluate a Web document located on a single Web page in a Web site. However, to do that successfully, students must place the document and page in the context of the site as a whole, which is why evaluation begins with general information and a concentration on ethos before moving to specifics (see Figure 6.3).

Figure 6.3   Critical Evaluation of a Web Site

Name:_____   **Date:**_____

CRITICAL EVALUATION OF A WEB SITE
SECONDARY SCHOOL LEVEL
©1996-2006. Kathleen Schrock

1. What type of connection do you have to the Internet?
   - ___ Dial-up connection: modem speed (circle one) 28.8 -- 33.6 -- 56k
   - ___ Direct connection: (circle one) 56K—DSL—T1—T3—Broadband/cable—other: _____

2. What Web browser are you using?_____

3. What is the URL of the Web page you are evaluating?

   http://_____

4. What is the name of the site? _____

Part 1: Technical and visual aspects of the page As you look at the questions below, put an X in the *yes* or *no* column for each.	YES	NO
Does the page take a long time to load?		
Do any pictures or photographs on the page add to the information?		
Is the spelling correct on the page?		
Are there headings and subheadings on the page?		
• If so, are they helpful?		
Is the page signed by the author?		
Is the author's e-mail address included?		
Is there a date on the page that tells you when it was last updated?		
• If so, is it current?		
Is the format standard and readable with your browser?		
Is there an image map (large clickable graphic with hyperlinks) on the page?		
Is there a table (columns of text) on the page? (Check the source code to be sure.)		
• If so, is the table readable with your browser?		
If you have graphics turned off, is there a text alternate to the images?		
On supporting pages, is there a link back to the home page?		
Are the links clearly visible and annotated or explanatory?		
Are there photographs or sound files on the page?		
• If so, can you be sure that a picture or sound has not been edited?		
• If you're not sure, should you accept the information as valid for your purpose?		

Summary of Part One
Using the data you have collected above, write a short statement explaining why you would or wouldn't recommend this site to a friend for use with a project.

_____

_____

_____

Part 2: Content As you look at the questions below, put an X in the *yes* or *no* column for each.	YES	NO
Is the title of the page indicative of the content?		
Is the purpose of the page indicated on the home page?		
When was the document created?		
If there is no date, is the information current?		
Does up-to-date information matter for your purpose?		
Is the information useful for your purpose?		
Would it have been easier to get the information somewhere else?		
Would information somewhere else have been different? • Why or why not?		
Did the information lead you to other sources, both print and Web, that were useful?		
Is a bibliography of print sources included?		
Does the information appear biased? (One-sided, critical of opposing views, etc.)		
Does the information contradict something you found somewhere else?		
Do most of the pictures supplement the content of the page?		

Part 3: Authority As you look at the questions below, put an X in the *yes* or *no* column for each.	YES	NO
Who created the page?		
What organization is the person affiliated with?		
Conduct a *link:* command in a search engine to see who links to this page. Can you tell if other experts in the field think this is a reputable page?		
Does the domain of the page (k12, edu, com, org, gov) influence your evaluation?		
Are you positive the information is valid and authoritative? • What can you do to validate the information?		
Are you satisfied the information is useful for your purpose? • If not, what can you do next?		
If you do a search in the newsgroups on the creator of the page, do you find additional information that shows the Web page author is an expert in the field?		

Narrative Evaluation

Looking at all of the data you have collected above while evaluating the site, explain why or why not this site is (or is not) valid for your purpose. Include the aspects of technical content, authenticity, authority, bias, and subject content.

VISUAL LITERACY CHALLENGE 2   ■

Web Sites and Evaluative Arguments

There are many other questions to ask about the documents, pages, and sites one encounters on the World Wide Web. However, an evaluation form with guiding questions provides a structure for a thorough rhetorical analysis of these items. After working collaboratively on the evaluation of a common Web site, students should test their skills on sites of their choosing. The teacher may use this opportunity to discuss different genres, beginning with the idea of an "educational Web site." What, for instance, makes a Web site educational? Is it the information on its pages? How does one define "information" on a Web page? Does one include graphics in that definition? This provides an opportunity for students to write a Why List (see Chapter 4) investigating ideas to discover their own beliefs, which are more than likely undeveloped. Afterward, the teacher may wish to assign an essay that offers an evaluative argument based on the students' examination of the Web site's rhetorical elements. This will demand critical thinking, drawing on a number of literacy skills, including those required for visual literacy. Here are some guidelines for that exercise.

What to Do

1. Ask students to choose a hypertext document and evaluate it based on three criteria (A, B, and C) that they establish. Their evaluative claim should use the following formula:

    X is (or is not) a good example of Y because it has (or does not have) features A, B, and C.

2. Tell students they can use any of the following suggestions to write their evaluative argument, or choose a topic of their own, provided that the subject of their evaluation is an online hypertext. Indeed, they may wish to evaluate whether:

    *   an "educational Web site" is (in)effective as an educational tool.
    *   a "government Web page" is (un)successful as a resource for its audience.
    *   a "nonprofit organization's Web document" is (in)effective publicity.
    *   a "business Web site" is (in)effective as an advertising tool.
    *   an "online essay" or "electronic magazine" is an (in)effective publication.

3. Share these writing tips with students:

Remember the value of controversy in your arguments. Your evaluation won't succeed if a preoccupation with graphics and special effects leads you to ignore the ethos and logos of the document, producing a thesis that stirs only agreement. Beware: Do not mistake style for content! Concentrate on the content of your hypertext document as much as its design and graphics.

Be sure your criteria for evaluation are appropriate to your subject, since you will have to establish their validity. For example, you may have to explain why the criteria you would apply to critique an educational Web site would be different from those you might apply to a business Web site. For suggestions on how to do this, visit "Evaluating Web Pages" (http://www3.widener.edu/Academics/Libraries/Wolfgram_Memorial_Library/Evaluate_Web_Pages/659/), an online guide written by researchers at Widener University's Wolfgram Memorial Library.

Be specific. The more you narrow your topic, the easier it will be to develop. It will help to have an audience in mind as well as a purpose. If necessary, create a scenario to help yourself. Imagine you are a consultant for a school, a business, or an institute that wants feedback on its newly designed Web site. Or, imagine you're a panelist at a conference on the future of publishing, and you have been asked to evaluate a hypertext—an online book, magazine, or essay—to determine the effectiveness of this new medium. Use your imagination, as well as your critical-thinking skills, and you'll find this exercise both stimulating and rewarding.

State your topic proposal. Your topic proposal should state your evaluative claim or thesis, explain why you think evaluating your subject is problematic, and describe the criteria you tentatively plan to use in your evaluation.

■ GLOBAL LITERACY

After studying the complexities of visual literacy—learning to see online documents as they are, not as preconceptions tell us they should be—students are better prepared for an even more ambitious literacy. This one speaks to the promise of the Internet, which is an "international network" of computers that enable telecollaborative learning activities. Behind the rhetoric inspired by the notion of a global village, however, lurks a series of challenges that are not for the faint of heart. To meet those challenges, teachers must be prepared to bring all of the previous literacies to bear, challenging students to stretch their limitations beyond municipal, state, regional, and national boundaries. In short, it is time for them to acquire global literacy. The only problem? How can teachers teach something that they have not learned themselves? How might educators design and facilitate telecollaborative learning activities that inspire global literacy?

7

Evaluative Literacy

Peer Reviews, Electronic Portfolios, and Online Learning Records

In every academic discipline, students need to acquire better understanding of their own learning style and process, as well as become better critics of their own work. Often, they suffer the delusion that it is acceptable for either the style or content of their work to be weak so long as the strength of its counterpart compensates for that weakness. This may be true occasionally, but, regardless of the academic discipline, students must become critical of both the style and substance of their work. Critical judgment is essential, for it helps them discover the flaws in their work, which is the first step toward the kind of evaluative literacy necessary for self-improvement (see Figure 7.1).

Figure 7.1

Evaluative Literacy

Evaluative literacy is the ability to distinguish excellence from mediocrity as it applies to both the process and product of one's labor.

Without knowledge of alternative approaches to a task, and without an understanding of the strengths and weaknesses of those approaches, students remain ignorant of the process that leads to a finished project, report, or essay. This, in turn, may lead to misunderstandings about evaluation because the euphoria that attends the completion of a project may have more to do with overcoming a flawed process than producing quality work. What's more, students often believe they can cut corners on the process and still arrive at a quality product. Sometimes they can, but what if they cannot? How can teachers demonstrate a good process approach to writing essays, reports, and more with new technology? How might they use networked computers to help students change their approach—refining their process—so that they can produce better quality work? How can educators teach students to turn a critical eye toward their own work, judging both its strengths and weaknesses? Ultimately, how can teachers in networked classrooms use technology to help students develop more evaluative literacy?

This chapter's literacy challenges and case studies respond to those questions, presenting a sequence of building blocks that become increasingly complex. First, the "Hypertext Writing Workshop" focuses on one draft of a written project. Next, "Electronic Portfolios" enables students to collect the respective pieces involved in a particular project, revealing both their process and final product. Finally, the "Online Learning Record," a hypertext collection of a semester's work, encourages students to select their best work, reflect on both the process and product, and offer a summative report and self-evaluation. Thus, the narrative moves from evaluation of a part to the whole, giving careful consideration to the process of learning, the quality of student work, and the evaluative skills necessary to understand the relationship between the two.

Let's begin with an exercise written for students, which guides them through an electronic variation of a tried-and-true method.

■ EVALUATIVE LITERACY CHALLENGE 1

The Hypertext Writing Workshop

What to Do

1. Share the following letter with students.

   Dear Writing Workshop Participants,

   To build a "community of writers" we need to help each other "see" our writing through another's eyes. However, this means we must learn to trust one another, as both readers and writers. When asked to critique someone's essay or report, you are helping them "re-see" their work. That is what *revision* means; literally, we "see again," but this time, hopefully, we see from a different perspective, one that improves our judgment. Your observations and comments will make a strong impression, so please be responsible and compassionate with them. This doesn't mean saying only nice things, but it does mean trying to "show and tell" what you're seeing so that the writer receives it as constructive criticism. If you work diligently at this, helping the writer improve, you'll develop the skills necessary to critique your own writing and strengthen your evaluative literacy.

In the past, peer-review sessions were usually conducted on paper, asking classmates to exchange papers, scribble notes in the margins, and circle typos and grammatical errors. How might we transfer this process to sessions in a computer lab? Where are the margins in which we write notes to the author? How do we highlight errors? How do we allow for more than one reviewer to comment on the style and content?

Actually, it's not that hard if you know a few HTML tags or work with a "WYSIWYG" (What You See Is What You Get) editor. Either way, a little ingenuity will allow you to call attention to troublesome words and phrases, highlight awkward sentences, and comment on confusing passages. This exercise will help you see what's going on inside an essay. It begins with close reading of a text. In fact, it asks you to give the text three close readings. This may seem odd, but with practice, you'll learn that rereading is essential to the process of "re-vision." You will have approximately 30 minutes for the entire exercise, so you'll have to budget your time well. And remember the golden rule: "Do unto others' compositions as you would have them do unto yours."

2. Instruct students that all editing will be done on a copy of the author's electronic draft, which means using HTML tags for notations. The authors should save a backup of their original draft as well as a review copy. Each review session will last approximately 30 minutes. Reviewers should work carefully through the essay, following the instructions below.

3. Participants will rotate by shifting two computer terminals to their right. They should work on the essay at that terminal for the first 30 minutes. Before beginning, remind reviewers to make sure the author saved his or her draft as "roughreview.html." This means they will be working on a separate copy of the text, not the original. On completion of the reviews, the authors can link to their reviews from the original, using it to guide revisions.

4. Tell students to use the following conventions:
   a. Wherever the instructions say to highlight something, they'll need to use the HTML tags or the menu bar of their WYSIWYG editor to accomplish the following:

   Reviewer 1: Highlight using boldface: Highlight = <B>BOLD-FACE TYPE</B>
   Reviewer 2: Highlight using italics: Highlight = <I>ITALIC TYPE</I>

   b. To indicate agreement or disagreement with their co-reader, they should follow these rules:

   If, as Reviewer 2, they disagree with Reviewer 1, they are to offer a comment at the end of the paragraph. If, as Reviewer 2, they agree with Reviewer 1, they are to use *italic type* on top of the **boldface type** to reinforce the concern.

For example, let's say they encounter a sentence like this: "The truth cannot be told by me."

Reviewer 1 finds this awkward, so he or she highlights it and offers a parenthetical comment:

"The truth cannot be told by me." **(Awkward)**

Reviewer 2 agrees, so he or she highlights the sentence as well and adds to the parenthetical comment:

"The truth cannot be told by me." **(Awkward—*Passive Voice!*)**

This will tell the author that both reviewers see a problem here and that the second reviewer offers a diagnosis. Remind students that neither reviewer is responsible for fixing the problem. Rather, they merely call attention to the problem, helping the author see the text through a fresh set of eyes.

What if Reviewer 2 disagrees with Reviewer 1? Then the highlighted item would appear in boldface, but not in italics. This indicates that the reviewers do not agree on the matter. Fair enough: The author will serve as final arbiter.

5. When instructed, everyone should shift to the next terminal on their right, serving as the second reviewer for the essay before them.

6. Tell students they should try to accomplish three major objectives in their three readings.

First Reading—Take Inventory: Ask students to take inventory in the first reading. This applies mostly to Reviewer 1, but Reviewer 2 should verify Reviewer 1's work.
   a. Underline the essay's claim and the reasons supporting it.
   b. Underline the "grounds" on which the claim and reason are founded.
   c. Underline the first sentence of each paragraph.
   d. Number each paragraph (chronologically) by placing a number at the start of it.
   e. Highlight typos and other "distractions."

(Reminder—Do not fix any of the mistakes; simply help the author see them.)

Second Reading—Evaluate the Basics: In the second reading, ask both Reviewer 1 and Reviewer 2 to evaluate the basics by accomplishing the following:
   a. Assess the thesis paragraph—Is it clear? Well supported? Does it indicate the direction the essay will take? Does the diction reveal

an awareness of audience? Does it hint at "conditions for rebuttal" or "qualifiers?" Type a brief comment at the end of the opening paragraph.

b. Transitions—At the start of each paragraph, judge the transition from the previous paragraph as "strong," "fair," or "weak." What do the underlined topic sentences at the start of each paragraph reveal about the structure of the essay? Where is it flawed?

c. Highlight confusing phrases, and write a brief comment in parentheses (i.e., "I'm not sure what you're saying here. Are you?").

d. Use the "strikethrough" command to draw a line through redundant words and phrases.

e. In the space below each paragraph, offer a brief commentary on the paragraph's weaknesses; let the author know if the prose is vague or confusing; suggest additional material if the support seems "thin." Be specific!

Remember: Reviewer 1, type your comments in **boldface**; Reviewer 2, in *italics*.

Third Reading—The Big Picture: Style and Structure: For the third reading, ask students to concentrate on the big picture—the style and structure of an argument. This applies equally to both Reviewer 1 and Reviewer 2.

a. After each paragraph, assess the author's use of supporting evidence. Is it persuasive? Is it documented properly?

b. Highlight errors with in-text citations, and offer a parenthetical comment on bibliographic documentation.

c. Critique each paragraph, referring to it by number. Tell what each paragraph says and does. Is it coherent? Does it show and tell effectively?

d. Prepare a final commentary. At the end of the essay, each reviewer should provide his or her full name, type a one-paragraph commentary that addresses the following questions, and save the document. Again, Reviewer 1 should type the commentary in **boldface**, and Reviewer 2 should use *italics*. Here are a few questions to guide responses:

Argument: Assess the strength of the author's claim and reasons. Is the author aware of his or her own assumptions? Does a lack of evidence undermine the author's ethos at any point? If so, where? Which point of the rhetorical triangle (logos, ethos, or pathos) should the author emphasize more (or less) in the next draft?

Structure: Overall, how do the reviewers like the structure of this essay? Would they move a paragraph to give it more prominence in the essay as a whole? Would they delete one altogether? Does the essay flow naturally from one paragraph to the next? Are the transitions graceful or forced?

Style: Where is the prose interfering with the argument instead of making it clear? Is the tone and voice of the essay appropriate for the audience that the author addresses? Is the documentation complete and reliable?

Suggestions: What, if anything, is missing from this essay? What needs the most attention in the next phase of revision?

Rather than isolate a peer-review sample, examining it out of context, let's see how this works in a process approach that integrates hypertext and portfolio assessment. By doing so, one can glimpse a number of advantages to conducting peer reviews as hypertext writing workshops.

■ CASE STUDY: ELECTRONIC PORTFOLIOS

As students learn to evaluate their peers' efforts and see their own work through another's eyes, they must also learn to transfer evaluative literacy skills to their own work. Toward that end, they need a strategy that encourages reflection on their research and writing processes, as well as a way to collect the disparate pieces of their work. Borrowing from the idea of portfolio assessment with printed materials, teachers can help students through this process by arranging electronic portfolios for a given project. Although this exercise grows out of language arts and humanities instruction, it is applicable to projects in most academic disciplines. It begins with the creation of a simple hypertext template that emphasizes research, reflection, and a process approach to writing. By constructing electronic portfolios, students create a record of their research and writing process, develop HTML skills, and strengthen their evaluative literacy.

What's the appeal of an electronic portfolio? Does this variation accomplish anything that print portfolios cannot? Certainly, this activity shares a good deal with its print cousin. For one thing, it provides context for student work. How often does a school curriculum encourage students to think in holistic terms, situating disparate learning activities and fragmented disciplines in a larger context? As a result, they often think of learning activities as "busywork" a teacher creates to keep them occupied, rather than as part of a coherent learning process. As much as anything, portfolio assessment tries to overcome this. The electronic portfolio, by extension, will help students think of their work not as an isolated essay or report for a particular teacher or class, but as part of a larger conversation—one that connects them with a community of scholars. The electronic portfolio process distinguishes itself from print variations because the medium allows students to link directly from their composition to online resources. Meanwhile, internal links between the respective portfolio sections encourage a self-conscious and reflective approach to composition.

To illustrate the importance of this type of approach, let's consider a common academic assignment: the research essay. Typically, the process goes something like this: The student chooses a research topic and submits a proposal that the teacher must approve. Then, the student conducts research, taking notes from secondary sources that will help support a particular argument (often a preconceived argument the research will merely reinforce rather than question). Finally, the student outlines an essay, writes a draft or two, and produces a final draft replete with citations and bibliography. Now stop to consider this process. How much time did the student spend reflecting on it? How much of the process has the teacher seen? How much of it will be reflected by the final draft? How much of the process does the student retain? Does the student see the relationship between that process and the final product, or has the obsession with that destination blinded the student to the journey?

The answers to these questions will depend largely on the specific students and teachers, but, generally speaking, the final draft of a conventional research paper reveals only a fragment of the process involved in its creation. With a portfolio, however, the final draft is placed in the context of the entire project. The electronic portfolio offers the unique opportunities of hypertext, which allows one to move through the internal links of the portfolio sections as well as depart from it to consider the secondary sources that informed the writer's thinking.

CASE STUDY: ONLINE LEARNING RECORDS   ■

Adapted from the California Learning Record, a portfolio model inspired by the Primary Language Record developed in Great Britain during the mid-1980s, the Online Learning Record (OLR) feels like a natural progression from peer reviews and electronic portfolios. Just as the electronic portfolio allowed students to pull the disparate pieces of a single project together, the OLR provides an opportunity to represent a semester's work, from postings on class mailing lists or discussion forums to transcripts of synchronous chats or asynchronous telecollaborations, as well as peer reviews, essay drafts, and more. In essence, the OLR allows students to showcase both the quality and quantity of their work while participating in the evaluation of their overall performance. Here is how one of its principal creators, M. A. Syverson (1998), describes its purpose:

> The Online Learning Record integrates research, assessment, and teaching and learning practices for computer-enhanced literacy development. The Learning Record provides a format for documenting student progress and achievement, based on interviews, observations over time, samples of students' naturally-occurring work, and well-supported interpretations of learning across five dimensions.

To accomplish these goals, the OLR asks students to provide the following information, which could be entered into a hypertext template that the teacher creates or an original, student design:

- Background information and data collection
- Summary interpretation of five dimensions of learning
- Self-evaluation

Selection of materials is left to the students' discretion, but by addressing these three fundamental concerns, they acquire privileged insight into their own process and the work that it produces. The teacher may choose to employ the OLR as a supplement to conventional assessment or use it as the only assessment tool, in which case students would submit an OLR at both midterm and end of term. What follows is a brief discussion of the respective sections and how they contribute to a student's evaluative literacy. Admittedly spare, this introduction cannot do justice to the OLR but should, at the very least, provide a thumbnail sketch that encourages teachers to learn more about this alternative assessment method.

a. Background information and data collection. As with the electronic portfolio, background information provides a glimpse of the student's personal and intellectual journey. However, it shifts the focus from the relatively short time span of a course project to the life span of the student. Teachers may choose to modify this section of the OLR to suit a particular discipline, but the fundamental prerequisite is a description of the student's development, as described by the student and someone who knows that student well. For example, in a humanities course, the teacher may ask that both the student and acquaintance describe this individual's development as a reader, writer, and thinker. This accomplishes several things, including self-evaluation, corroboration from another, and privileged insights into an individual's history as a student. More important, it situates the present work in the context of personal history, helping both the student and teacher gain critical perspective.

The second part of this section, data collection, presents two important elements: observations and evidence of work. Similar to process journal entries, the observations offer short, informal responses to readings, class discussions, and online activities. They are not the activities, but reflections on them. As such they constitute a "meta-level" narrative, encouraging students to step back from their work to periodically reflect on their reactions and assess the impact of particular learning activities. The evidence of work section, meanwhile, provides students with an opportunity to select representative samples of their best work. The selection process itself forces students to evaluate their work, deciding which pieces deserve a place in this online showcase. There are three principal categories from which to choose:

- Samples of written work—writing exercises that culminate with a final draft (topic proposal, rough drafts, etc.), electronic portfolios, and so forth.
- Samples of comments by others—e-mail messages from the class mailing list, discussion forum postings, peer reviews, and so forth.
- Samples of other activities—e-mail exchanges through the class mailing list, postings in the class discussion forum, excerpts from synchronous discussions, and so forth.

Obviously, these categories could be amended to suit different disciplines, while their present form leaves them open to a range of interpretations. What is essential, however, is giving students an opportunity to select their best work, demonstrating the quality of their effort and performance through a variety of materials that might otherwise be forgotten due to their ephemeral nature.

b. Summary interpretation. The temptation for students who are new to the OLR is to leap from data collection to self-evaluation. However, they should resist that temptation, for it neglects an essential step in the process: summary interpretation. As its name suggests, this segment of the OLR will ask students to interpret their performance. To do so, they must isolate individual strands of work and interpret them along specific learning dimensions. For students in a rhetoric and composition course, Syverson (1998) recommends the following breakdown:

Four major strands of work: Rhetoric, research, technology, and collaboration.

Five dimensions of learning: (1) confidence and independence; (2) knowledge and understanding; (3) skills and strategies; (4) use of prior and emerging experience; and (5) reflection.

Students may choose to write this summary as a lengthy paragraph or break it into disparate pieces, dedicating a paragraph to each of the major strands (and their learning within them). This, too, is left to the discretion of the students and teacher. Regardless of the form the summary takes, it's important to impress on students the significance of this segment of the OLR. At both midterm and end of term, this summative interpretation draws on the observations and evidence of work highlighted in Part A, considering them with respect to the four major strands of work and the five dimensions of learning. This is not busywork, but a prerequisite to a thoughtful self-evaluation in the final section of the OLR. Having selected exemplary work and reflected on their learning experiences, students are ready to apply evaluative literacy skills to the final topic: themselves.

c. Evaluation. On completion of the previous sections—and not before—students evaluate their performance. At the midterm, this requires looking forward and backward, simultaneously assessing the work they have accomplished while stating resolutions for the remainder of the semester. The OLR encourages students to offer suggestions for improving the course, from new learning activities to a change of pace or classroom dynamics. This provides students with a sense of ownership while demonstrating the teacher's interest in their input. It is important that the teacher take these ideas seriously, either by addressing proposals in a brief narrative response or by acting on them, altering the classroom activities and environment. Otherwise, students will lose interest in the exercise, viewing it as a meaningless ritual. Much the same applies to the final requirement of the midterm evaluation: an estimation of their work in terms of a letter grade.

At the end of term, this section of the final OLR spends more time looking backward than forward, though students are welcome to offer the teacher suggestions for future classes. Based on the previous sections, as well as supplementary information, students evaluate their work in terms of a letter grade. This feels strange to many students. Some will balk, others will underestimate their performance, and some will reveal an inflated sense of accomplishment. However, each response invites dialogue with the teacher, who can use the opportunity to help the student evaluate his or her work more objectively, demonstrating respect for the student's efforts and evaluative judgment while articulating the principles that inform the teacher's assessment. While this may seem awkward initially, it transforms the "grading game" into a rhetorical exercise. The teacher must not allow students to offer an unqualified assertion: "I deserve an A." Rather, students must make an argument based on thoughtful criteria and careful consideration of the ethos, logos, and pathos of their semester's work.

■ PEDAGOGICAL LITERACY

While much of this chapter's discussion focused on the development of student literacy skills, the respective exercises and case studies—the Hypertext Writing Workshop, electronic portfolios, and OLRs—will undoubtedly affect teachers as well. By engaging in alternative assessment, the teacher challenges conventions, which provokes questions about the strengths and weaknesses of various assessment methods. Portfolios deliver far more insights into student processes than teachers acquire through a conventional final draft of an essay, report, or project. In most cases, this breaks down barriers between the student and teacher, encouraging a more collaborative environment. However, changes in assessment methods often prompt changes in pedagogical approaches. Thus, one needs to consider the teacher's role more carefully. This explains the focus of the final chapter, pedagogical literacy.

8

Pedagogical Literacy

Plugging Into Electronic Pedagogy

It seems appropriate to conclude this discussion by considering pedagogy as a form of literacy. How so? In ancient Greece, the *paidagogos* was a slave who escorted children to school. Thus, pedagogy was composed of all the tricks employed to accomplish that task. One can only imagine the trials suffered while trying to get rebellious youngsters to obey. Indeed, pedagogy required skill in "reading" the child's disposition, writing a plan of action (syllabus) that would fulfill the objectives (curriculum), and articulating that plan in a persuasive manner (rhetoric).

Despite technological advances, modern educators have much in common with the ancient *paidagogos*. Today's educator must learn to read learning styles and write syllabi that fulfill mandatory curricula culminating with standardized examinations. The introduction of computers and networked technology hardly simplifies matters. In fact, it often complicates them. While integrating new technology, therefore, educators must continually ask which forms of literacy they value most and how technology might help students acquire it. To accomplish this, the classroom practitioner needs to become fluent in various technologies, learning how to read their strengths and weaknesses. Then, depending on the age group, learning styles, and curriculum of the students, educators must determine when to use these tools and when to set them aside. This constitutes pedagogical literacy, a fluency with the strategy and tactics we can employ along with networked technology for educational purpose (see Figure 8.1).

Figure 8.1

> ## Pedagogical Literacy
>
> Pedagogical literacy is a fluency with the methods that one can employ for teaching and learning as well as the critical judgment necessary to determine which activities and media are most appropriate for a particular group, time, and purpose.

The pedagogically literate teacher draws on a wide range of skills while developing an instructional repertoire. Only through a demanding process called praxis, which Paolo Freire (1997) described as a combination of "reflection and action" (p. 107) can we arrive at a point where our rhetoric and action, our means and our ends, form a coherent system. This requires periodic detachment and critical thinking about the choices we make, from our rhetoric and actions to the literacies we've inspired. Though it makes us uncomfortable, we as educators must hold a mirror up to nature to see what has happened to ourselves and our schools along the way.

After all, not every use of computer technology enhances the learning environment. Not all pedagogical strategies succeed all of the time with all of our students. Nonetheless, how can educators determine whether something will work if we never give it a try? How will we acquire computer literacy, or a sophisticated degree of pedagogical literacy, if we never try to develop our "vocabulary" and understanding? We must move at our own individual pace, starting from a comfort zone that allows us to transfer skills acquired with one medium to that of another. As always, our colleagues prove instructive, particularly those who define the extremes of the pedagogical spectrum. With that in mind, this final chapter presents two illustrative cases: first, the traditionalist who refuses to try new gadgets or practices, then, an experimentalist who flourishes when tinkering with the status quo.

■ MR. WYNEGAR'S PASTIME: TRADITION AND THE INDIVIDUAL TEACHER

Technology alone will not save teachers from weak pedagogy or literacy skills. We've learned this from experiences with one technology or another, often learning to simplify because we let the technology dictate too much of the activity in our classroom. After all, pressing "play" on a VCR hardly qualifies as thoughtful pedagogy, though pressing "stop" at a critical moment to heighten suspense and inspire speculative discussion might!

Teachers would do well, therefore, to remember traditional approaches even as they experiment with new ones. Every educational institution has its share of dedicated teachers who have succeeded without depending on electronic technology to teach literacy skills. For centuries, students have learned about reading, writing, and speaking from these people, traditionalists like Mr. Wynegar, who taught for nearly 40 years. He was rather fixed in his ways, for they served his students well. He was also fond of his idiosyncrasies, including a profound hatred of the word *very*. So great was his disdain for this adverb that when he returned student compositions, their stationery sported rectangular holes, the result of tiny scissors clipping the offensive adverb from every sentence where it appeared. Some would argue this was not a very professional response. It was not the kind of behavior one might learn in a course on, say, the methodology of writing assessment.

Still, it was effective.

Why? Perhaps because it was so unprofessional. Perhaps because it had so much personality to it. Perhaps, just perhaps, because it was so human.

Most students felt fortunate to have Mr. Wynegar as their English teacher. He taught them a lot about word choice, sentence structure, the mechanics of writing, and the personality of language and people. He also had a good point to make about the word *very*, and his method for making that point, unconventional and quirky though it was, made a lasting impression. Students would never forget holding their essays up to the light and finding them riddled with more holes than a colander. They would frequently shove a returned essay into a notebook without letting others see it, but their furtive glances confirmed what they knew instinctively: They had much to learn about writing. While they might never reach Mr. Wynegar's extreme in their writing style, they had to respect the conviction those scissored perforations represented.

More important, though, they admired the strength of personality, the courage, that those perforations revealed. Mr. Wynegar was not afraid of being unconventional; he didn't care what those holes said about his personality, nor what his colleagues might say about his teaching methods. Unlike many educators, he knew that teaching began as the expression of personality and ended as an escape from it. Unfortunately, the evolution of teaching in this century makes one wonder how much room is left for personality in the classroom. While teachers pay lip service to the craft of teaching, the emphasis on outcome-based learning, standardized tests, "plug-and-play" software packages, and Internet connectivity threatens human exchanges in their classrooms. Critics of these trends argue that

> the work of teachers has been increasingly subject to the rationalizing logics of management. The results have been the de-skilling of teaching with its accompanying loss of control over the activity of classroom life, an over-standardization of curricula and teaching, an introduction of management ideologies and techniques that may be utterly inappropriate in an education that aims at promoting democracy in more than name only. (Apple, 1990, p. x)

One explanation of such developments, which signal a shift from art to science and the attendant concern for objectivity, is the educator's desire for professionalism, a magical commodity that some believe will secure the respect that has often eluded educators. While the pursuit of professionalism pleases administrators, school board members, and a society obsessed with appearances, it does not guarantee effectiveness in a classroom. In the zealous rush to professionalize educators (borrowing the conventional definitions of that term from other fields, in particular, the corporate world), the gain in objectivity is offset by a loss of personality in the classroom and humanity in our schools. Objectivity is often a Pyrrhic victory, however, for while it invests educators with professionalism, it separates them from those with whom they must establish a more personal, individual relationship: their students.

Teaching, particularly in the K–12 classroom, cannot be divorced from a teacher's personality. Regardless of how many education courses one may take in classroom management, child psychology, or teaching methods, the teacher's professionalism will be useless if it overwhelms the personality that must convey it. Teachers would do well to remember the counsel of a flawed educator who failed to practice what he preached: "To thine own self be true." A music teacher with a sense of humor should not attempt seriousness at all times. Students see through this. They know when teachers are not being true to themselves. They lose respect for the teacher who is phony and become indifferent to those who seem diluted in character, shadows of a previous, more lively self. This is not to say that a sudden break from character is ineffective, as when a soft-spoken teacher quiets an unruly group with an unprecedented raising of the voice, just that "faking it" or repressing one's true character are recipes for disaster in the classroom.

The best teaching, like the best writing, occurs when one allows for spontaneity. Writing that follows a strict guideline, never deviating from a syllabus or lesson plan, may be efficient, economical, and persuasive, but it often feels contrived and uninspiring. The same applies to teaching. Teachers encumbered by an outline, pressuring themselves to cover everything before the bell rings, are likely to lose sight of the students before them. Teachers who commit themselves to the material more than the human beings in the classroom are making a mistake. This transforms them from human beings into automatons who refuse to let anything distract them from their syllabus. Course objectives, little notes in a black book, will satisfy their professionalism, but at what price? We need to think of professionalism in new terms, encouraging teachers to experiment with pedagogical strategies, deviate from rigid curricula, and challenge their students intellectually without stifling personality—either their own or their students'. Contrary to current trends, perhaps the most professional thing teachers can do is resist the impulse to standardize and objectify their pedagogy and classroom demeanor. Standardization and objectification are counterproductive in an environment in which each student deserves to be treated with the dignity and respect his or her humanity demands.

The analogy between teaching and writing helps illustrate the importance of not only having personality, but also knowing how to use it for didactic purpose. In his celebrated essay, "Tradition and the Individual Talent," T. S. Eliot (1978) claimed that "it is not in his personal emotions, the emotions provoked by particular events in his life, that the poet is in any way remarkable or interesting" (p. 506). By substituting *teacher* for *poet*, one may gain a sense of the analogy's force. Do not be deceived by Eliot's words, however. He argued that poetry is an escape from emotion and personality, though not the dissolution of it. The writing of poetry, like the teaching of children, demands clear expression of emotions and ideas, though not necessarily unique emotions or ideas, which Eliot claimed would only "discover the perverse." It's important to understand the prerequisites to such an escape, by either poet or teacher:

> Poetry is not a turning loose of emotion, but an escape from emotion; it is not the expression of personality, but an escape from personality. But, of course, only those who have personality and emotion know what it means to want to escape from these things. (Eliot, 1978, p. 507)

What this means, really, is that teachers must use all their human qualities—from vocal inflection to facial expression, cognitive ability to emotional response—to educate. In so doing, they express a personality that gives shape to ideas, much as the artist's craft gives shape to thought and emotion. This leads to one of life's paradoxical truisms: By offering the personal anecdote and allowing one's own vision to give shape to a curriculum, one discovers the universal through the personal. This is what Eliot (1978) meant by the individual's "escape from these things." If teachers do not take risks, sharing something of themselves and their interests, their quirks and contradictions, the very things that make human beings human, what chance is there that young students will gain a sense of humanity from schools? Students who reflect on great teachers often recall what was original and unique about them. In a word, what gave them, and their classes, such "personality." Critics of this argument may call it egocentric, but they miss the point. With apologies to Mr. Eliot, one could argue that teaching "is not a turning loose of emotion, but an escape from emotion; it is not the expression of personality, but an escape from personality" (p. 507). And yes, "only those who have personality and emotion know what it means to want to escape from these things" (p. 507), to push beyond their own limited definitions of the self and the rhetoric used to construct that "self," to engage the universal.

Mr. Wynegar knew what it meant to escape from personality and emotion, but, unfortunately, he never took that final step. By the time he retired, leaving the school where he had taught for nearly 40 years, he had become a caricature of his former self, a man more renowned for his idiosyncratic teaching strategies than a dynamic personality. He had, in effect, become an extension of his pedagogical routines, rather than making his pedagogy the extension of a dynamic self. Do we really want this to happen to our teachers? Do we really want to make schools and curricula "idiot-proof" by reducing education to strategies and tactics that are to be replicated by "guides on the side" who avoid the expression of individual personality? Shouldn't we encourage teachers to keep growing, challenging themselves and their students to search within themselves, their personal interests, emotions, and beliefs, to discover the universal? Failure to do so will produce a generation of people who are strangers to themselves, detached from emotions and human society.

Society owes a great deal to people like Mr. Wynegar, educators who passed the "sacred fire," not only to young students who would eventually become writers, but also those who went on to become teachers of reading and writing. We learned a great deal from teachers like Mr. Wynegar. However, current trends in education, particularly the embrace of technology that displaces the teacher, promoting the guide on the side while dismissing the "sage on stage," may signal yet another triumph of technique over humanity, science over art, and professionalism over personality. For all those idiosyncratic quirks and all the remarkable strategies he employed—from standing behind a podium to snipping adverbs from student essays—were initially an expression of Mr. Wynegar's personality. Unfortunately, they eventually became an end in themselves; the tools Mr. Wynegar had shaped for performing his craft eventually shaped him in ways he hadn't foreseen.

What educators need is encouragement to continue growing and learning, reinventing themselves and their practice. Early in his career, Mr. Wynegar knew this without articulating it. That individual possessed what one educator described as "knowing-in-action," a wisdom that is hard to classify, yet indispensable:

> When we go about the spontaneous, intuitive performance of the actions of everyday life, we show ourselves to be knowledgeable in a special way. Often we cannot say what we know. When we try to describe it, we find ourselves at a loss, or we produce descriptions that are obviously inappropriate. Our knowing is ordinarily tacit, implicit in our patterns of action and in our feel for the stuff with which we are dealing. It seems right to say that our knowledge is in our action. (Schön, 1995, p. 29)

Mr. Wynegar had a "feel" for what he was doing, as well as "the stuff with which [he was] dealing." At least, he did before he became a slave to his own conventions and his idiosyncratic methods stunted his personality. At the start of his career, he had an intuitive feel for the classroom and the courage to teach universal lessons through personal expressions. Though he'd bridle at the use of an offensive adverb, he was a very good teacher because of those expressions.

■ MS. SABADILLA AND THE ELECTRONIC CHALKBOARD

And now, a word on behalf of innovators, those who wish to experiment with new technology and pedagogical strategies. Despite the ways in which they differ from Mr. Wynegar, many of these people, particularly those who work in the humanities, share a belief he espoused for decades: The art of writing is rewriting.

Teachers of language arts chant this mantra during composition workshops. Ironically, though, these same instructors have often resisted the use of computer labs for facilitating workshops. Initially, many in the humanities pledged allegiance to the Luddites, describing the word processor as an instrument of evil in the hands of a young writer. Extremists called for the prohibition of computers in language arts instruction because they feared students would develop a harmful dependency, using technology to check spelling, grammar, and other fundamentals, instead of refining their skills.

While one might understand such concerns, even empathize with them, they remain as reactionary as the protests of humanists in the 16th century who feared the adoption of printed texts would destroy the memory of students. In the 20th century, teachers of mathematics expressed a similar anxiety when they claimed the use of calculators would prevent students from developing fundamental skills and the mnemonic devices that had supported the study of their discipline for centuries. In recent years, teachers have seen how uncoached word processing can harm the writing of secondary students. Weaker students sometimes do confuse the appearance of a manuscript with its content, believing justified margins, a spellchecker, and sleek fonts hold the secrets to a first-rate essay. However, it shouldn't take more than one set of papers to disabuse them of this fallacy. Then, if one really wants to use the word processor to advantage, the real fun begins.

Despite its drawbacks, the word processor is the best tool for editing prose ever invented. It's that simple. Ms. Sabadilla worked as a journalist in college. She enjoyed writing articles, but she loathed editing on hard copy. She had learned to type articles and essays in triple space, allowing room for editing marks. By the time an article was done, it looked like a road map, though instead of interstate highways running at all angles, grease pencil corrections sprawled across the page. It wasn't until she graduated from college and began teaching that word processors became common, revolutionizing the editing process forever.

Now, as a high school journalism teacher, Ms. Sabadilla uses the computer as an integral part of her teaching, particularly the teaching of composition skills. Some of her colleagues still take perverse pleasure (or is it pride?) in declaring that they know almost nothing about the computer and have no desire to learn about it. She wonders what they would say, though, if one of their students expressed similar feelings about whatever topic they were teaching at that moment. Open-minded folks interested in improving their instruction of writing and editing skills, however, may find her experience enlightening.

For years, Ms. Sabadilla slaved over essays that repeatedly contained the same mistakes. She scribbled "awkward" in margins, crossed out unnecessary words, and often retyped sentences or paragraphs that were in special need of editing. This required loads of time and usually did little to improve the next set of papers. The only exercise that seemed helpful to the class as a whole was writing sentences out on the chalkboard and asking students to revise them. In some cases, though, the chalkboard was not big enough to accommodate a full paragraph, or else her penmanship was not good enough to make the exercise efficient.

Then Ms. Sabadilla discovered the digitized projection screen, or liquid crystal display (LCD) panel. This device, when placed atop an overhead projector, was the magic wand she'd been seeking for writing and editing workshops. The digitized projection screen allows one to insert a disk with writing samples into a word processor, open a file, and immediately project it onto a screen or wall for the entire class to see. Ms. Sabadilla likes to select half a dozen paragraphs from student essays, type those onto a disk, and collate all the paragraphs onto one sheet, which she prints out and copies for her students. The paragraphs, perhaps the introductions or conclusions of essays (without names attached), are then distributed to the class. Students are directed to edit the paragraphs as carefully as possible, removing unnecessary words or clichés, improving awkward word choices, and generally tightening and clarifying the paragraph as a whole. After they have had time to do this on paper, they are ready for a collaborative session at the projection screen.

This is when the technology feels like magic. At this point, the teacher has an opportunity to do more than tell students what should or shouldn't be done; he or she has the chance to show them how to go about editing and revising. The effort is a collaborative one that involves the entire class, not just a single student who may or may not understand cryptic notes in the margin of a paper. What is especially good about using the computer for this exercise is that one can save different versions of the same paragraph, including the original, for comparison after everyone is satisfied with the editing. The advantages of this technology over the traditional chalkboard should be obvious, for the latter becomes an enormous road map of insertions, cross-outs, and chalk smears, obliterating the original paragraph entirely by the time a single paragraph is edited.

Most important, the innovation of an electronic chalkboard introduces new possibilities for teaching and learning. Writing teachers can usually edit several times as much work on the computer as they could on the traditional chalkboard in the same class period. With a computer and digitized projection screen, teachers spend more time editing and discussing the virtues of a good sentence and far less time with the mechanics of assembling a sentence for student inspection. They also discover—and invent—a wide range of learning activities that the conventional chalkboard never enabled. In Ms. Sabadilla's class, for example, students now use the LCD panel, along with a computer connected to the Internet, to offer hypertext presentations, review online articles, and analyze the rhetorical impact of Web sites.

■ ELECTRONIC PEDAGOGY: THE WEB SITE

Mr. Wynegar deserves respect for his high standards and steadfast commitment to principles, pedagogy, and pupils. However, Ms. Sabadilla's innovations are equally commendable and merit respect for the courage and convictions they require. Of course, not all innovations are good, for some are simply "improved means to unimproved ends." However, one example of a positive innovation when it comes to teaching literacy skills is the shift from a slate chalkboard to a digitized screen. Mr. Wynegar never tried using one of these, though he did employ an overhead projector from time to time. Perhaps the LCD panel came along too late in his career, at a time when his skills and practices had been honed to such an extent that to alter his pedagogy would have required a profound alteration of himself.

It is worth noting that Mr. Wynegar retired several years ago, prior to the push for integrating networked technology into school curricula. He never had to learn about meaningful, instructional uses of computer technology. Perhaps this was just as well for Mr. Wynegar, but it's not an option for many of today's educators. The extraordinary effort to connect classrooms to the Internet has placed a tremendous burden on teachers.

Unfortunately, expenditures on infrastructure have not generated similar expenditures on the people charged with the mission of introducing electronic pedagogy to their curricula. Because of their limited professional development opportunities, educators need a place to learn about electronically supported, pedagogical tools.

It should go without saying, but let's say it anyway: Telecomputing is not about computers. It's about educating our students, serving our communities, and improving our societies. If it's not about those things first and foremost, it has no place in our curricula. Indeed, this book sprang from the hope that a discussion of literacy in the Digital Age would inspire reflection on the critical literacies fundamental to a well-rounded education: media literacy, civil literacy, discourse literacy, personal literacy, community literacy, visual literacy, global literacy, evaluative literacy, and pedagogical literacy. It is now up to students and teachers to define a more meaningful and satisfying form of computer literacy. Here's hoping this book contributes to that cause—one teacher and several students at a time. To do so, it must inspire further dialogue and pedagogical innovation, which are necessary to discover—and invent—improved means for helping 21st-century students become truly literate individuals.

Appendix: Index of Web Sites

Web Site Name	URL	Cited in Chapter
All Search Engines	www.allsearchengines.com	2
Beyond Portfolios: The Learning Record Online	www.cwrl.utexas.edu/~syverson/olr	7
Center for Democracy & Technology	www.cdt.org	2
Classroom Connect	www.classroomconnect.com	2
Computer Professionals for Social Responsibility	www.cpsr.org	2
Computer Writing and Research Lab	www.cwrl.utexas.edu	2
CPSR Cyber-Rights	www.cpsr.org/cpsr/nii/cyber-rights/index.html	2
European Computer Driving Licence Foundation	www.ecdl.com/	2
Glossary of Internet Terms	www.matisse.net/files/glossary.html	2
Hobbes' Internet Timeline v8.2	www.zakon.org/robert/internet/timeline/	2
Internet 101	www.internet101.org	2
Internet Public Library: Citing Electronic Information	www.ipl.org/div/farq/netciteFARQ.html	2
Kathy Schrock's Guide for Educators	school.discovery.com/schrockguide/	6
Learning Record	learningrecord.blogspot.com	7
Learning Record Online	www.cwrl.utexas.edu/~syverson/olr	7
Learn the Net	www.learnthenet.com/english/index.html	2
Ohio University: Free Speech	www.ohiou.edu/esl/project/freespeech/index.html	2
Onion, The	http://www.theonion.com	6
Plato: The Republic	http://classics.mit.edu/Plato/republic.html	3

References

Apple, M. W. (1990). Series editor's introduction. In *The new literacy: Redefining reading and writing in the schools.* New York: Routledge.

Berger, J. (1972). *Ways of seeing.* London: Penguin.

Bolter, J. D. (1991). *Writing space: The computer, hypertext, and the history of writing.* Hillsdale, NJ: Lawrence Erlbaum.

Classroom Connect. (1994–1995). Acceptable use policies: Defining what's allowed online and what's not. *Classroom Connect Newsletter.* Available from http://www.classroomconnect.com

Costanzo, W. (1994). Reading, writing, and thinking in an age of electronic literacy. In C. L. Selfe & S. Hilligoss (Eds.), *Literacy and computers: The complications of teaching and learning with technology.* New York: Modern Language Association.

de Castell, Suzanne A. L., & Maclennon, D. (1989). On defining literacy. In A. L. Suzanne de Castell & K. Egan (Eds.), *Literacy, society and schooling: A reader.* Cambridge, UK: Cambridge University Press.

Eisner, E. (1985). *The educational imagination.* New York: MacMillan.

Eliot, T. S. (1978). Tradition and the individual talent. In A. W. Litz (Ed.), *The Scribner quarto of modern literature.* New York: Charles Scribner's Sons.

Gergen, K. (1991). *The saturated self: Dilemmas of identity in contemporary life.* New York: Basic Books.

Gibaldi, J. (1999). *MLA handbook for writers of research papers* (5th ed.). New York: Modern Language Association.

Graff, G. (1990). Other voices, other rooms: Organizing and teaching the humanities conflict. *New Literary History, 21,* 817–839.

Haas, C. (1996). *Writing technology: Studies on the materiality of literacy.* Mahwah, NJ: Lawrence Erlbaum.

Landauer, T. K. (1996). *The trouble with computers.* Cambridge, MA: MIT Press.

Lanham, R. (1994). *The electronic word: Democracy, technology and the arts.* Chicago: University of Chicago Press.

Liddell, H. G., & Scott, R. (1973). *A Greek-English lexicon.* Oxford, UK: Oxford University Press.

Lunsford, A. A., Moglen, H., & Slevin, J. (Eds.). (1990). *The right to literacy.* New York: Modern Language Association.

Lunsford, A. A., & Ruszkiewicz, J. J. (1999). *Everything's an argument.* Boston: Bedford/St. Martin's.

Myers, M. (1996). *Changing our minds: Negotiating English and literacy.* Urbana, IL: National Council of Teachers of English.

New Shorter Oxford English Dictionary (Vol. 3). (1993). Oxford, UK: Clarendon Press.

Papert, S. (1993, June). *Obsolete skill set: The 3 Rs.* Retrieved August 6, 2007, from http://www.wired.com/wired/archive/1.02/1.2_papert.html

Plato. (2000). The Republic. In *The Internet encyclopedia of philosophy.* Retrieved August 6, 2007, from http://classics.mit.edu/Plato/republic.html

Postman, N. (1993). *Technopoly: The surrender of culture to technology.* New York: Vintage.

Queneau, R. (1981). *Exercises in style* (B. Wright, Trans.). New York: New Directions.

Ramage, J. D., & Bean, J. C. (1998). *Writing arguments: A rhetoric with readings* (4th ed.). Boston: Allyn and Bacon.

Rheingold, H. (1993). *The virtual community: Homesteading on the electronic frontier.* New York: Addison-Wesley.

Schön, D. (1995, November/December). Knowing in action: The new scholarship requires a new epistemology. *Change,* 27–34.

Shakespeare, W. (1964). *The sonnets.* New York: Signet.

Syverson, M. A. (1998). *Beyond portfolios: The learning record online.* Retrieved August 6, 2007, from http://www.cwrl.utexas.edu/~syverson/olr/

Talbott, S. L. (1995). *The future does not compute: Transcending the machines in our midst.* Sebastopol, CA: O'Reilly & Associates.

Turkle, S. (1997). *Life on the screen: Identity in the age of the Internet.* New York: Simon & Schuster.

Further Readings

Anderson, D., Bret, B., & Paredes-Holt, W. (1998). *Connections: A guide to online writing.* Boston: Allyn and Bacon.

Ba, M. (1986). *Scarlet song* (D. S. Blair, Trans.). Harlow, UK: Longman.

Barton, D. (1994). *Literacy: An introduction to the ecology of written language.* Oxford, UK: Blackwell.

Brewer, B., Davis, H., & Jeutonne, P. (1997). *Electronic discourse: Linguistic individuals in virtual space.* Albany: State University of New York Press.

Bump, J. (1990). Radical changes in class discussions using networked computers. *Computers and the Humanities, 24,* 49–65.

Burniske, R. W. (1998). The shadow play: How the integration of technology annihilates debate in our schools. *Phi Delta Kappan, 80,* 155–157.

Burniske, R. W. (1999a). Computer illiteracy: Vice or virtue? *AFT on Campus, 18*(5), 18.

Burniske, R. W. (1999b). The teacher as skilled generalist: Preserving humanist traditions in an age of technological utopianism. *Phi Delta Kappan, 81,* 121–126.

Burniske, R. W., & Monke, L. (2001). *Breaking down the digital walls: Learning to teach in a post-modem world.* Albany: State University of New York Press.

Edgar, C., & Wood, S. N. (Eds.). (1996). *The nearness of you: Students and teachers writing on-line.* New York: Teachers and Writers Collaborative.

Getzels, J. W. (1982). The problem of the problem. In R. M. Hogarth (Ed.), *Question framing and response consistency.* San Francisco: Jossey-Bass.

Gilster, P. (1997). *Digital literacy.* New York: John Wiley.

Graff, H. J. (1995). *The labyrinths of literacy: Reflections on literacy past and present.* Pittsburgh, PA: University of Pittsburgh Press.

Harris, J. (1998). *Virtual architecture: Designing and directing curriculum-based telecomputing.* Eugene, OR: ISTE.

Hirsch, E. D. (1987). *Cultural literacy: What every American needs to know.* Boston: Houghton Mifflin.

Hutchins, E. (1996). *Cognition in the wild.* Cambridge, MA: MIT Press.

Kling, R. (Ed.). (1996). *Computerization and controversy: Value conflicts and social choices* (2nd ed.). San Diego, CA: Academic Press.

Lave, J., & Wenger, E. (1991). Situated learning: Legitimate, peripheral participation. In J. F. B. Roy Pea (Ed.), *Learning in doing: Cognitive and computational perspectives.* Cambridge: Cambridge University Press.

Lipman, M. (1991). *Thinking in education.* New York: Cambridge University Press.

Messaris, P. (1994). *Visual "literacy": Image, mind, and reality.* Boulder, CO: Westview Press.

Ong, W. (1982). *Orality and literacy: The technologizing of the word.* London: Methuen.

Plato. (1980). Imitations of Horace, Epistle I. In E. M. Beck (Ed.), *Familiar quotations.* Boston: Little, Brown.

Selfe, C. L., & Hilligoss, S. (Eds.). (1994). *Literacy and computers: The complications of teaching and learning with technology.* New York: Modern Language Association.

Snyder, I. (Ed.). (1998). *Page to screen: Taking literacy into the electronic era.* New York: Routledge.

Tuman, M. (Ed.). (1992a). *Literacy online: The promise (and peril) of reading and writing with computers.* Pittsburgh, PA: University of Pittsburgh Press.

Tuman, M. (1992b). *Word perfect: Literacy in the computer age.* London: Falmer Press.

Tuman, M. C. (1987). *A preface to literacy: An inquiry into pedagogy, practice and progress.* Tuscaloosa: University of Alabama Press.

Tyner, K. R. (1998). *Literacy in a digital world: Teaching and learning in the age of information.* Mahwah, NJ: Lawrence Erlbaum.

Warschauer, M. (1999). *Electronic literacies: Language, culture, and power in online education.* Mahwah, NJ: Lawrence Erlbaum.

Willinsky, J. (1990). *The new literacy: Redefining reading and writing in the schools.* New York: Routledge.

Windschitl, M. (1999). The challenges of sustaining a constructivist classroom culture. *Phi Delta Kappan, 80,* 751–755.

Wordsworth, W. (1979). My heart leaps up. In M. H. Abrams (Ed.), *The Norton anthology of English literature.* New York: W. W. Norton.

Index